MW01087986

FIRST-HAND ACCOUNTS FROM THE
UKRAINIAN FRONTLINE

FIRST-HAND ACCOUNTS FROM THE
UKRAINIAN FRONTLINE

OKSANA MELNYK

Pen & Sword
MILITARY

AN IMPRINT OF PEN & SWORD BOOKS LTD.
YORKSHIRE - PHILADELPHIA

First published in Great Britain in 2024 by
PEN AND SWORD MILITARY
An imprint of
Pen & Sword Books Limited
Yorkshire – Philadelphia

ISBN 978 1 03611 150 2

Typeset in Times New Roman 12/16 by
SJmagic DESIGN SERVICES, India.
Printed and bound in the UK by CPI Group (UK) Ltd.

Pen & Sword Books Limited incorporates the imprints of Archaeology,
Atlas, Aviation, Battleground, Digital, Discovery, Family History, Fiction,
History, Local, Local History, Maritime, Military, Military Classics, Politics,
Select, Transport, True Crime, After the Battle, Air World, Claymore Press,
Frontline Publishing, Leo Cooper, Remember When, Seaforth Publishing,
The Praetorian Press, Wharncliffe Books, Wharncliffe Local History,
Wharncliffe Transport, Wharncliffe True Crime and White Owl.

For a complete list of Pen & Sword titles please contact:
PEN & SWORD BOOKS LIMITED
George House, Units 12 & 13, Beevor Street, Off Pontefract Road,
Barnsley, South Yorkshire, S71 1HN, England
E-mail: enquiries@pen-and-sword.co.uk
Website: www.pen-and-sword.co.uk

or

PEN AND SWORD BOOKS
1950 Lawrence Rd, Havertown, PA 19083, USA
E-mail: uspen-and-sword@casematepublishers.com
Website: www.penandswordbooks.com

MIX
Paper | Supporting
responsible forestry
FSC
www.fsc.org   FSC® C013604

CONTENTS

Introduction

FIRST-HAND ACCOUNTS FROM THE UKRAINIAN FRONTLINE

When Russia's full-scale invasion of Ukraine began, analysts around the world gave Ukraine three days to survive the threat. But the country held out. What helped Ukraine resist the terror of the aggressor, whose territory occupies one-seventh of the planet's landmass?

Here are the stories of Ukrainians who rose up to defend their country during the Russian invasion of Ukraine. Some of the narrators had never held a gun before the full-scale invasion, while for others it was a profession.

These stories are about human action, excruciating pain, exhaustion, and grief, but above all, about everything we love and cherish. These stories are also about those who are no longer with us. They are about who we are apart from being ordinary people, students, workers, priests, teachers, farmers, doctors, professors, managers, actors, artists, rock stars, pensioners, parents, children, and so on.

These stories are not just about armed people, they are about warriors. If some weapons help to resist the Russian invasion and survive, other weapons help the courage to live on. You can find it in the words of all these people and arm yourself with it, whoever and wherever you are.

FIRST-HAND ACCOUNTS FROM THE UKRAINIAN FRONTLINE

Chapter 1

FIRST TIME

Narrator Pylyp Dukhliy is an electronics technician and business manager by education. Co-founder of the #Brobots project (technical training), a full-time school in Kyiv, robotics studios for local authorities, and distance courses in programming and robotics.

I met Johnny during training before going to the front, and we just clicked. Johnny is the call sign of my fellow in the army; he is Ukrainian. I have never met a more stubborn, and yet dependable, person in my life. Johnny is always composed and remains calm, no matter the circumstances. Really, what does he have to worry about if he cannot hear what holy shit is going on around us? Maybe the reason why he is such a nice and friendly guy is that he also doesn't hear other people around him.

Johnny is a really good electrician. Before the war, he worked in France and Germany. As soon as everything started, he returned home to join the army as a volunteer. Johnny was deaf in one ear and had no more than 30 per cent hearing in the other one. Constant shelling made things even worse, and his hearing aid no longer helped.

When we approach the frontlines, Johnny follows close behind me, watching to see when I drop to the ground to avoid incoming fire, so that he could do the same. Occasionally he gets distracted and remains standing under the whistle. I've got used to grabbing and pulling him to the ground with me. Sometimes I tell him stories, but his reply is about something completely different. We have got used to that and joke about it. So ironic that we are both in the communications unit…

One night, Johnny was on lookout duty. Rachyk – the call sign of a guy from our unit – walked past him on his way to pee, but Johnny soon forgot about it. When Rachyk came back a little while later, he almost shit his pants after Johnny held him at gunpoint and nearly shot him. After that, we didn't ask Johnny to be the lookout.

We nearly died yet on our way to Avdiivka's direction on the frontline.

We didn't have time to find out that the emergency exit at the back of our bus was blocked when it came under mortar fire. I was the last one to enter that bus and should have been sitting in the back. Somehow on this day, Johnny happened to save a seat for me in the third row near him.

When the explosion hit, we jumped through the windows and front doors, falling on the ground, and covering our heads while debris was falling all around us. Our ammo detonated inside the bus shortly after the mortar fire began.

Those who were sitting behind were burned alive and injured. Some people in the back of our bus were severely wounded in the attack. One of us, who was sitting in the back of the bus, did not get through in the nearest medical unit after his leg had been blown off. He sustained massive blood loss and died with no final words. When I later was lying under the rubble during the missile attack, I remembered the bones and skulls of those who just were too far from the door. Boys who just couldn't get off that bus.

These were the first months of the full-scale invasion.

We all were overwhelmed with rage. Seven other buses were struck at the same time. Nobody told us where we went. We didn't have bulletproof vests and helmets on. Our command was warned that the enemy expected us to move on that road.

I was not afraid of death, but of the process of dying. I was afraid to wait for the unknown. Sitting in the dugout and counting the approaching mines. To think whether the dugout will hold off the next one, because it whistles and sounds like it is almost right here.

Step on the paw of a dog hiding inside. To have a smoke. The dog yelps to the rhythm of the mine whistle. Under that yelping, a mine falls somewhere nearby and explodes. Screaming, swearing, and yelling everywhere. A pile of stones at the entrance to the dugout and no counter-battery work – it appeared in about two months after we had come to the frontline. The multiple missile launcher system did not work. We had only twenty-five shell mines for responding fire – almost nothing.

We had to work under the whistle of bullets, but I loved going to work on the communication line. Leaving the cold and dark dugout, breathing in fresh air and sunshine made me wish to live again. My companion and I would lie down on the grass, smell the cold fresh air, close our eyes, and listen to the birds. There were only fifteen minutes of light and bullets started to whistle again.

The light was too dosed. We could stay in the dugout for a long time. We could only see and hear what was happening right in front of our eyes and ears. We did not know what was going to happen next, as if everything we were doing was useless, and we were just waiting to be killed.

When we were told that we inflicted the enemy losses, it was like a ray of light in our infinite informational vacuum. It turned back to life as if we were lying on the grass under the sun for fifteen minutes.

Some people's bladders or intestines could not withstand the shelling, while others learned to sleep soundly even during the shelling. I didn't sleep well and used to wake up when the sky was just starting to turn grey with no sun rays. This is the east – it dawns there around 4.00 am. Plus, I used to get up very early for the morning toilet. It was a risky event in the daytime.

When I came back to the dugout, I would wake up Father, my fellow priest in peaceful times. Our first time in that position he stayed for nights there, but when the mine's whistle became closer and louder, he started to come to the common dugout. Here, Father was our cook. I didn't like him right away. When the war broke out, he took a vacation and a weapon. We would go to his kitchen to drink coffee. Father is a kind man, but sometimes he could quarrel like the devil and bless us with a scolding or even a hit with his ladle.

The kitchen was his temple, and it was crucially ascetic. In the morning, he would make a pot of tea, cut bread with sausage and cheese, and open canned food. For lunch, he would make borsch or soup. For dinner, we mostly ate porridge with stew.

There was a catastrophic shortage of meat. Once a young roe deer ran near one of the positions and our guys shot it. Father gutted and cleaned it, and, in the evening, we had a barbecue.

It was quiet on Easter Day. Father gathered us in the kitchen, took out candles and prayer books, and put the Easter cakes we had received from the volunteers on the table. He held a service. We listened to him and were baptized. Then Father was taken to another unit. He received two contusions. His kitchen was hit, and it's gone. And I still have a wooden cross and a prayer before going to bed.

A mile from the frontline, it is impossible not to believe that God exists. Too much depends not on you, not even on the people around you. A shell hits a trench in the ground, and somehow debris does not fall at us. A mine with a top detonation falls nearby and does not explode. Dozens of mines with thousands of darts that can turn a human body into jelly... The guys are sitting in a dugout opposite each other, and a piece of ammo flies right between them. Just a little closer to one side or another and somebody's wife could become a widow. A sergeant major, who came to take our guys to the infantry yesterday, was crushed by a slab. He was here talking to us absolutely alive.

When we received our first salaries (it was the biggest salary in the army as we were near the frontline), I asked the guys about the choice issue. What would they do? Would they go home or stay here with great financial prospects? No one chose the money. We left our home on patriotism, but got there on seven shelled buses.

There were almost no healthy people in our unit. Stomach ulcers, heart attacks, hypertension, lumbar hernias, missing fingers, pancreatitis, contusions... I asked about going to the medical unit when my heart started to fail during shelling.

When a missile hit the building of that medical unit in a village club, I was sleeping inside. Maybe I lost consciousness instantly and did not hear the explosion.

I was sleeping under the wall on my side, not my back or stomach, and that's why I stayed alive. A piece of the wall fell over me and it covered a bed with me like a dome. The fragments of the building were falling on this dome. I was in shock, but not in pain. I was alive.

Also, I could stay alive as it was not my first time dying and I saved my consciousness. Dissociation is a defence mechanism of the psyche that does not allow signals to process. When it happens for the first time, even ordinary human fear cannot break through the shell of dissociation. When you live you're dying many times, the pain threshold increases, and immunity appears.

A fire was crackling nearby, and people were running around looking for the wounded. I heard voices and was sure that I was about to be found. I was screaming for a long time and finally realized that I could burn alive, and everything would be over. My phone, documents, cards, helmet, armour, everything I had – burned; only pants, T-shirt, and underwear remained. Time and space were swollen like a balloon. Not five minutes passed, but an eternity.

The fire spread and people's voices were getting quieter. Some guy's intestines were taken out. Another had brains visible through a smashed head. Some had their hands completely burned. Those people were sleeping about 20 metres (65 feet) from me. A little more time and the ammunition would have started to explode. I was saying goodbye to my life and screaming when realized that I was the last to be pulled out. I walked barefoot over the debris and glass and felt no pain.

When I came back home after the hospital, all my flowers had dried up, except for the indoor bamboo. I watered them for a long time in the hope that they would revive. So strange, isn't it? Aimless hope that life will be the same again...

When I start to touch what I have hidden inside me, it touches me back with my tears and cold sweat. It squeezes my throat from the inside. I returned from the war only physically. A part of me is still there, but I brought the war to my home in my heart. It always sheds light on things that used to seem a farce but are not something valuable.

Taking a shower. Cooking something delicious. Walking in the park. Waking up in the middle of silence in fresh sheets. Going to bed in the evening. Meeting friends and talking about jobs and self-development. Loving. Hugging. Living another day. Probably this day is not as sunny as you expected. But you have a chance to live that until the end not only for you, but for all the Earth.

Chapter 2

TO FIRE THE GALLEYS

The narrator of this chapter is Volodymyr Rashchuk, a film and theatre actor and unit commander in the Svoboda (Freedom) Battalion. He went to defend Ukraine from the Russians without any combat experience. Volodymyr, call sign Actor, took part in heavy battles in Donbas, including the fight for Severodonetsk, the temporary administrative centre of the Luhansk region, while part of it was under occupation. After heavy fighting from February until June, the nearly destroyed city came under Russian occupation.

If the Lord had set a goal to create humans as immortal, he would not have started with Adam. The line of immortals would have started with George. Serhiy Zherzhevskiy, who had the call sign George, survived even the Ilovaisk cauldron. Ilovaisk took hundreds of lives, but George is one of those who were captured by terrorists and was lucky enough to return from captivity.

George did not look like someone who once could be killed. It was he who reignited the spirit of freedom amongst our boys when we held Severodonetsk city.

'Guys, to be honest, I am done. Leave me wounded, dead, cooked, anything', George said to me and my comrade Beard.

Beard and I together transported food and ammo across the bridge. I was the unit commander; Beard was the platoon commander. George was commanding on his own on the other side of the bridge, and it was really challenging for him. But he didn't leave Severodonetsk.

Ingrained in George was the belief that the human spirit could not be broken, and they had to continue the resistance even here, the abandoned place with almost no buildings. George was almost on the verge of burning out, as he shared this spirit, leaving nothing for himself. It is very important always to keep something for yourself. I am a professional actor, so I know what I am talking about.

When an actor steps on the stage, he must be full of life because the audience is there seeking a cure. During an accident in an aeroplane, you must put the mask on yourself first, and then on the child. Imagine a typical audience. The person sitting in the third row might be thinking about some work issues. Someone's car has broken down in the sixth row. A bunch of people in the tenth row have had their salaries cut. Sex issues and problems with kids plague everyone in the second row. Some wives in the fifth row have just learned that their husbands have mistresses. And the lady at the end of the hall has real trouble – she's figured out that her bestie is more attractive than her.

People come to the theatre to forget their problems. There are 750 seats, the hall is full, and you must be ready and prepared to give all they want. It is disappointing if these people do not get what they came for. But it is even worse if, after you leave the stage, you are unable to go home, be a good husband and father, walk your dog, feed your cat and just be yourself. Life ends when you don't have enough left for yourself.

George was mortally wounded in the chest and neck during contact combat. We hoped that everything would be fine. But when George was gone, Beard and I began commanding the company. We were surrounded, and I talked face-to-face with almost 100 soldiers.

'Actor, I really want to see you at least today and tomorrow', said Sam. He came to me, crying.

'Are you nuts? Don't you need me two days from now?' I tried to squeeze out a joke.

'I don't know what will happen to us', he said.

'No one knows, my little brother. But we always find a way out. If there is a firefight, we will take it on. We need to fight to save as many lives as possible.'

Sam was a student who dreamed of becoming a professional arborist. He even completed a special course in Sweden in January 2022. He was like a real little brother to me. He married his girlfriend two weeks before the world lost him. Sam died during an air raid near Severodonetsk. Before the outbreak of full-scale war, he planted a sprout of a ginkgo tree – a tree that does not die. After his death, this tree was transplanted to the Kyiv Botanical Garden. Sam was only 22.

Those who romanticize the war are the same people who think that men don't cry. My T-shirt was constantly wet, but not from sweat. We were losing people who meant more to us than our brothers and sisters – even more than our parents.

My father called me from Donetsk, the city that was occupied in 2014. That year, he decided to stay.

'Can you use the proper Russian language when talking to me? You damn defenders.'

'Father, you need to leave Donetsk. When we come to Donetsk, you will be my enemy.'

My friend Kardan heard that talk. We smoked a lot together and discussed films about the Second World War. I regret having parts in such films. There is nothing accurate about the real war in that film.

We also lost Kardan in Severodonetsk. I have not talked to my father since.

Anyway, a lot of what happened was my fault. I threw my piece of wood into the Russian imperial bonfire, which did not disappear anywhere after the collapse of the Soviet Union. I used to work in a Russian drama theatre in Kyiv and acted in Russian-language films. I only gave up speaking Russian on 24 February 2022. I tried to smooth out the sharp corners when my wife Viktoria, a very conscious and exclusively Ukrainian-speaking patriot, added fuel to the fire during conversations with my father.

I'm from Mariupol and now my family has nothing left in that city. There, I even almost lost my sister. She managed to escape from the famous drama theatre in Mariupol five hours before the Russians dropped a bomb on it – despite the inscription 'CHILDREN' on the ground.

I paved my way to the east when I dismissed the idea of war. My wife talked a lot about that.

'We should buy a weapon. We need one.'

'Honey, just stop… that's impossible. How can I buy a weapon? I only touched that one on the film set…'

'Look around. Don't you see?'

'You should have got married to a captain, not a semi-man like me.'

In Severodonetsk city, we hardly ate and slept and did not wash for a month. We were nourished and cleansed by revenge. But revenge is a fast carb. It gives a powerful charge of energy when your brother is dying in front of your eyes. Revenge gives animal strength when even hatred has exhausted itself. There is only a pure goal to destroy, but it cannot last long.

But what is 'long'?

Once I did not sleep for three-and-a-half days, and it no longer felt like an hour, a minute, or a second. Every time some of our boys died, time stopped. It always stopped when I realized I might be next. There, I was the most vulnerable male on the Earth, but not because of my wounds and contusions and my constant flu.

Once, I came back from my lockout duty at the factory, which was one of our bases. I lay down and slowly drifted off to sleep, only to be awakened by the barely audible hiss of my sleeping bag's zipper opening.

It would be very poetic to say that I thought she was in my dream. But we have been together for a long time, and I know this woman so well. My wife, Viktoria, is someone who can come to see me even in the middle of Hell.

My Achilles' heel stood in front of me, and it was beautiful and terrifying at the same time. On the one hand, I was incredibly happy to see her. On the other hand, my beloved was *here*. I didn't know how she would get out of here.

When I argue with her, it always ends pretty much the same.

'Imagine that one of us dies. Does the problem exist in this case?'

'No, dear.'

I don't understand when men say, 'I fell in love.' I can't fall in love once and for all – I do it every time I look at her. She is also an actress, and now she is even more beautiful than she has been in any of her roles. The dimples on her cheeks, the corners of her lips, the curves of her eyebrows – even exhausted from the hard road and constant work, she still became more beautiful than ever.

She was with me for half an hour and left. I calmed down only when she left far enough to stay safe.

When I came back home after the Severodonetsk campaign, she told me that night that I went to our daughter, almost in a dream, and asked where the Russians were.

Upon arrival, my wife and I decided to quickly prepare a performance of *Romeo and Juliet* for my tired war buddies. I could not learn the text; my memory had deteriorated a lot. A friend of mine was afraid that I might lose more than my ability to memorize.

'I hope that the child that was in you before the war is still alive. You might become callous and cold. Seems like everything is okay', said my fellow director.

I understood what he was talking about. There is nothing human about war. For you to survive, someone else must die. It is the lowest level of relations between homo sapiens: the struggle for food, survival, power, dominance, and aggression. The penultimate day in Severodonetsk, we destroyed many of Ramzan Kadyrov's mercenaries. I was eager to scalp Shaman, a close friend of his.

We were ordered to leave the city but, on the way out of Severodonetsk[1], we knew that we would come back to fire our galleys.

In 334 BC, during the Phoenician campaign, Alexander the Great noticed from the shore that the enemy's army was three times larger in number. His soldiers gave up. Alexander gave the order to burn the ships on which he and his army sailed. They watched the burning ships with horror, realizing that the only way to get out of there was to use the enemy's ships. If that was not done, there was no chance to survive – to see their family, beloved woman, or children again. The soldiers understood Alexander's decision. The Macedonian army won and returned home on the enemy galleys.

Chapter 3

JELLY AIR

The narrator, named Nazar, decided not to fully disclose his identity. Nazar says that his identity doesn't need to be specified, because there are a lot of guys like him. He is a Ukrainian, so he fought once, he is fighting now, and he will fight all his life.

So, this is a parable about three friends. Listen up.

There was one small but courageous Ukrainian battalion of volunteers that was reinforcing the brigade of the Armed Forces of Ukraine in one of the Donetsk spoil heaps.

And there were three loyal friends in that battalion. They always kept together, but one day two of them took up defensive positions while the third one remained at the checkpoint.

Had those boys had more weapons to repel the assault, the whole situation would have turned out differently. The Russians mounted a powerful assault. They had tanks and many heavy guns, including D-30 howitzers, rapids, grads, smerch, cassette mortars, and phosphorus missiles. Everything was flying everywhere, reminiscent of fireworks on the Independence Day. 'Chandeliers' were hanging in the sky like Chinese lanterns. Those were round fiery mines with parachutes that lit up the sky a square mile for the Russian 'Orlan' drones. 'petals', small high-explosive mines that do not kill, but can make one a burden to society, were actively falling. They make a poetic sound, 'f-i-i-i-u-u-u', and fly like maple seeds. You could lie next to your trench and cover yourself with foil – you should always have foil in case it rains, even if it's summer and you are in the desert. Admire these firework shows and make a wish, like it's your birthday. If you're lucky enough to stay alive, this day may literally become your second birthday.

Anyway, our boys only had the 80-calibre mortar and the 120-gun without the ammunition and did not have cannon artillery then. The enemy positions were only 100 metres (260 feet) away. Radio handsets didn't work.

Brave friends were carefully moving away from the spoil heap towards the checkpoint. They did not feel joyful as they passed the position of some old fart from the Armed Forces of Ukraine with a weapon. That man saw somebody coming from the enemy side, didn't understand who it was, and started firing like there was no tomorrow. Some died from his fire, while at the same time the enemy kept firing rounds non-stop. This is not unusual: friendly fire is common in any war. But that's not the point of the story.

The second of our three friends was moving at the head of the group. They caught hell from the crazy old fart, fell wounded, completely lost their bearings, and started crawling in the wrong direction.

The third friend who remained at the checkpoint was trembling. He begged fellows with drones to find his friends. He cried a lot. He seemed not to find his place at the checkpoint.

The drones found the bodies of the two friends 20 metres (65 feet) from the Russian positions. Those friends had been in such a state of shock that they confused the geography and had crawled towards the enemy's positions.

So, here's the main thing. Those two wounded friends managed to crawl quite far. At the very edge of the abyss, each found the strength from within to help the other one. They both did everything to break a mathematical rule and make one plus one equal more than two. They kept dragging each other forward, pulling each other's arms and shoulders, pushing each other's sides. At some point, the strength of one of them gave out near the door of the abandoned factory they had managed to reach. The other one stopped moving as well.

Maybe they thought that they had reached their destination and that someone would open the door and get them on stretchers.

Perhaps they were closing their eyes one after the other. Maybe one of them closed the eyes of his friend.

Probably they are still lying next to that door.

Perhaps their third friend could not find his place not only at the checkpoint. By all indications, he looked like a person who would never find it anywhere on Earth.

I'm kidding.

This is not a parable.

And I don't know if the third one ever came back from the spoil tip. I, for one, barely made it out of there – although I didn't make it out of there 100 per cent.

The three of us – me, Softie, and Doc – led the group and returned to our positions. It was terribly dark that evening. We couldn't get flashlights as it would be the signal for the Russian 'Orlan'. We walked only along a trodden path, where on the way there and back we amused ourselves by neutralizing the 'petals' on the sides of our path.

Suddenly, a car passed by. It's impossible to tell who it was while it's 0.5 kilometre from the Russian position and the same distance from ours. Initially, we moved to the side to take up a firing position.

I stepped on a 'Petal' and flew off. The guys were carried away by the blast wave.

Later, in the hospital, I asked them to remove that stinking tunic from under my head. It stank of fried iron and rotten wheat. I was evacuated in a car that takes the dead from the frontline. I tried not to close my eyes. Because when you close your eyes and see nothing, you have nothing but that smell. You don't see the remains of people around you. You don't feel the wetness of blood. You only have this smell and your own weak breathing. It's like your own smell. There is no one else here...

I started to doubt whether I was still alive.

The first month after the explosion, I had very bad eyesight. After a concussion, you can't see the centre, only the picture on the sides. I could not hear well and had constant headaches. But then I felt the smells even more. Smells were everything to me. I could smell the evacuation vehicles even after the surgery...

A girl came to one guy in the hospital and brought him food. She opened a tray at the other end of the ward, but I could smell it all as if it was under my nose. The perfume on girls who came into the ward was like they were pouring buckets of that smell on themselves. I was like a service dog.

I survived; it happens sometimes.

If I could walk now, I would go back to the battlefield. This is the best war in the world, the most technological, bloodthirsty, and unprincipled. I have something to compare with. Nowhere else in the world are there such moods as on the frontline in Ukraine. Nowhere else is it so scary – I know what I'm saying, I'm the scary guy. Nowhere else is there so much driving force to fight. I am sure that if these people had only sticks and no weapon, they would throw those sticks at the Russians…

Before the Donetsk landfills and 'petal' fields, I was wandering in the Kharkiv direction. One hellish morning – 4.00 am near Barvinkove village in the Kharkiv region can only be hellish – the company commander was giving very serious orders.

'How many tanks do we have?'

'Five tanks at this position, all are problematic.'

'Write down all the problems on a piece of paper!'

Now, while I'm in the hospital, all these situations seem ridiculously funny to me. They are acceptable for understanding only *there*. Because only one tank was working properly – the rest in various combinations either did not move, or their barrel did not rise, or the turret did not rotate, or all of this together, but there was a possibility to fire.

The company commander's voice sounded like music. Those were beautiful sounds. They flew into our ears and spread throughout our bodies. Because when you realize that this is probably the last thing you will hear in your life, it becomes music and makes you break into a smile, no matter what you hear.

'You take this position and shoot as the barrel moves because the turret does not rotate, and the tank does not move. Don't move anywhere! When you run out of ammunition or you are hit, you get out of the tank and run away.'

The commander did not seem to be giving orders...

'You turn the turret, moving the tank as much as possible. And then you shoot.'

He was preaching.

'You at the third tank roll back to this position', he pointed to the map, 'and shoot from there and don't move anything.'

He approached the guys and looked into their eyes.

'There are women and children behind us. We must get into tanks and defend our homeland. If we don't do it here and now, no one else will.'

His words were not just convincing.

After the commander said about the last tank the tension in our basement was so strong that it could be eaten with a spoon.

'Guys, you are our only hope. You have to drive between the cowsheds and just shoot in that direction. Let them think we have a lot of equipment! Don't look where you are shooting, don't aim, just shoot in the direction of the enemy. Create an illusion!'

A quiet, choleric calm reigned there. The unjustified euphoria of victory reigned there. By God, I got a little hard-on, I'm sorry. I was thinking about how cool you all are here, guys, and how powerful you are...

People got into those broken tanks, driving the occupiers from their land with great fanfare, dying, and getting wounds. Later, a friend of mine further lifted the veil of the absurdity of everything that was happening there. It turned out that these were trophy tanks because at that time all our equipment was broken.

Yes, I would go there again if only to smell the jelly air of those basements. (My friend Softie brought me a flashlight, which I gave him along with the grenade so that it wouldn't get lost. Sometimes I take it out of the ziplock bag and take a deep breath. I recognize diesel fuel, soil, black bread, gunpowder, burning wood, and the incomparable, unique smell of weapons. This is *my* smell. I will not confuse it with anything else.)

The same morning, when we had a tank triumph, the commander of a reconnaissance battalion of a very good brigade brought very bad news.

'A huge convoy of Russian vehicles with a huge number of Russians is coming towards us. It will pass on the right side of the fork in the road. A special group is being assembled to move to the enemy's rear and create an ambush', he says.

The left side of the road was still ours; the right side was not. I joined the group. I don't know what I was thinking at the time, but I generally tended to agree with all sorts of nonsense. For instance, on the fourth month in a supine position, I thought, why on Earth I agreed to keep my leg? If I had agreed to an amputation, I would be learning to walk on a prosthesis.

A couple of guys and I volunteered, and we were given Javelins, rockets, and batteries. I held one for the first time in my life.

'Calm down, Dragon, I brought the instructions for the Javelin', said one guy from our group.

Dragon is my call sign.

'Come on, I'll read it while we're sitting in ambush.'

The brigade reconnaissance in that group went first. We, as a group with heavy weapons, went second. The first ones were supposed to report to us on the radio where and how far to move on.

They did not get in touch. Two minutes later, we heard shots from the forest so loud that we all froze.

'What are we doing?'

'We're just sitting here for now.'

'And who is "putting out" whom?'

'Not clear.'

Everything was working there, from grenades to machine guns. One of the reconnaissance group members got in touch.

'Don't move towards us, wait here. We ran into an ambush on our own.'

We gathered all our heavy weapons and took them to the road. We waited for the reconnaissance group. The group commander was killed on the spot, and the machine gunner was injured. Not all of us returned to the checkpoint.

That was my jelly air Sunday, 17 April 2022. At the checkpoint, somebody gave me a piece of Easter cake and a barbecue. Yes, it turned out that Sunday was Easter Day. While I was chewing, I decided to have a small talk with God.

'Listen, Lord, today some woman will get the news that her husband is in the gully forever. Their children will be told that their father is no longer alive. Tell me, Lord, why did everything turn out so clueless? Why today?'

But when the food hit the bottom of my stomach, I calmed down a bit.

'Whatever', I thought. We gave up that village anyway...

Shortly after that Easter morning, I was called to fight in some other area, and I left there. It is a great advantage of being a volunteer. You don't have to sit in one place and look at the same faces. The same people, the same tasks. You can do everything at the call of your heart. Not out of love, but at the call of the soul.

Somewhere in the semi-torn forests on a frontline I washed, changed my clothes, and went to the fire. There were huge guys, looking like bulls, sitting there with broken ears and noses. Their faces were such that you could break bricks with them. So, they were embarrassed of me looking for a place near the fire so relaxed.

'Do you even know who we are?'

'Of course, I don't.'

'We are bandits.'

'Hah, don't get your hopes up. You are not bandits.'

'But we've already served ten years in prison...'

'You are not bandits. Because the bandits have authority and wear dinosaur skin boots. Moreover, you are also victims of the political regime.'

'?'

'Because life makes you take such risks to earn your bread. You are not maniacs, and you do not like what you do. You do it because life makes you do it. Somewhere else in the world, you could be working in an office or as a sports coach, taking a sandwich tray with you, and having a wife and two cute children...'

'Well, yeah...'

The guys looked down at the ground.

My friend received a large dose of war exposure back in 2014. Now he lives and works abroad. He says that the hospital bed I am now confined to is my only chance to survive this war.

'If you had been lightly wounded, you would have recovered and run back to the war. Contusions and light shrapnel wounds would have kept you away for a month. If you had been hit again, you would have run to the hospital and done it again. Then you would have been brought in that evacuation vehicle only dead. Someone somewhere decided that it was not time for you. You must keep living.' I tend to believe him.

Chapter 4

AZOVSTAL

This is the story of Mykhailo Vershynin, the head of the Donetsk Oblast Patrol Police. After being wounded in the port of Mariupol, Mykhailo was evacuated to a hospital at Azovstal, a steel plant on the shores of the Azov Sea with a complex system of deep underground shelters and communications. The fighting at the Azovstal garrison lasted from 18 March to 20 May. As a result of the fighting, the plant was almost destroyed.

It was possible to get to Azovstal only at night. The maritime guard brought ammunition to the port by boat and took away the wounded people. On 7 April, I was evacuated with my wound to the position 'Zalizyaka' ('piece of iron'). That's what a military hospital there was called. Even then, Azovstal looked like hell as only the human imagination can paint it. Ammunition, water, and medicines were running out. I was lucky to get to 'Zalizyaka' when they were still operating under anaesthesia.

The surgeon cut off a piece of me, sewed me up, tied my left arm to my body, and ordered me to stay in the hospital. An injury like mine doesn't heal well, but I didn't feel too sick and went to the bastion. That's where Azovstal's command centre is, where I can be useful. And that's where I met Redis[2] and other commanders of the Azovstal garrison.

On 11 square kilometres (4 square miles) of Azovstal, the Russians had exploded enough ammunition for two Hiroshimas. Tactical and strategic aviation operated daily. There were always at least three Tu-22M3s. One day we counted sixteen of them: four for cover, the rest were bombers with ten to twelve half-tonne bombs or one FAB-3000 with 3 tonnes of TNT. These scum flew to Azovstal, bombed, and flew back. Later, the Russians began to terrorize Ukraine from the Caspian Sea.

Azovstal's shelters are designed to withstand different impact forces. However, the bomb shelter, which is located between the workshops under a four-storey building, jumps up when the FAB-3000 is blown up. Ship artillery, drones with bombs, and mortar attacks are then perceived as something ordinary and easy to get used to.

The explosions of strategic aircraft cannot be confused with anything else. Floors of bricks are stacked inwards like a house of cards. A mushroom of dust grows over the pile of bricks. Medical masks inherited from the Covid pandemic helped to protect us from the dust. (They helped a lot. I even took two masks, put them together, poured antiseptic on them, wiped myself, and was more or less clean.)

Several times we met helicopters loaded with medicines, thermal imagers, batteries, ammunition, and people who stayed here to fight and treat the wounded. On the way back, these helicopters would pick up the wounded. It was one of Azovstal's riskiest special operations. People had to overcome 100 kilometres (62 miles) of blockade to get there.

I had a conversation with the pilot of one of these helicopters. I said to him, 'You were psychopaths...'

He replied, 'You were the ones who were psychopaths – those who stayed at Azovstal...' This pilot, a very young guy, died later.

People are eager to pick up epic stories, which has done us a disservice. Azovstal turned into a reality show. News of helicopters with equipment flying over the sea to Azovstal spread at the speed of light. The Russians were outraged by this and started hunting for these helicopters.

One day I had to put the wounded in four helicopters. Everyone was worried, wanting to escape and looking for a free seat. Two of these helicopters were shot down.

I'm more than sure that the bunker point on the bastion was 'leaked' to the Russians. The headquarters was blown to smithereens. There are no such accidents: it arrived exactly where Redis usually sleeps at 2.00 am.

I fell asleep and very soon woke up from the explosion. Everything that was 1.5 metres away from my feet was destroyed. There were clouds of dust, concrete was falling. The soldiers were living out their last minutes. Inhuman screams mixed with the sound of the generator. Less injured people tried to help the more injured. The bomb swept everything away with them: thirteen dead.

Redis's friends were trapped under the rubble. He tried to move the slabs somehow, but they were too heavy: it was impossible without a jack.

It was getting harder and harder to carry the wounded on the Ironman. The Russians realized what kind of location it was and shot through all the entrances to the hospital. When they shelled Shop-20, another point for the wounded, seventy people died, burning alive. The Russians realized the target and did everything they could to neutralize it.

The 'big land'[3] constantly talked about the de-blockade of Mariupol. Like, we have already repelled the attack on Kyiv, and now we are breaking through to you guys, we are almost there... I could hardly contain myself so that people around me did not think I had gone mad.

Azovstal became the only centre of defence of the city. The depth of the blockade around it was increasing. The 36th Marine Brigade attempted a breakthrough and fell apart. About 180 people, led by Serhiy Volyna from the 36th and the remnants of the Azov Regiment, went to Azovstal.

There can be no de-blockade. It would take five to six brigades. The depth of the encirclement is more than 100 kilometres (62 miles).

Hope for salvation, if not supported by anything, turns into a small torture chamber inside yourself: you are the only one to blame for believing.

The defence of Mariupol could have ended much earlier than it did. If Redis had been sleeping on the bastion at 2.00 am that night, he would have been killed instead of leading the exit from the right bank to Azovstal. After the strike, we lost connection at the bastion, and he went to work at *'Zalizyaka'*. 'Eagles' with thermal imagers were hovering over the columns and firing indiscriminately.

Some things were repaired, some were not, but that exit was bloody. People were trying to get from the right bank to Azovstal through an iron bridge with a hole in it after an air strike. The guy on the armoured personnel carrier (APC) didn't see it, and they plunged into the water. Several people from the landing party survived, and another dozen people were unable to open the doors and drowned in the APC.

There was a KrAZ truck behind. It had every chance of passing by the hole in the bridge, but suddenly the driver jumped out of the car and just ran away. He was followed by other vehicles, from which people also spilled out in all directions. After that crossing, our scouts went around and picked up weapons, 'secret documents', and stuff from those cars.

People were crossing in rafts and boats. They swam in their gear, fell into the water, and did not have time to take anything off. Khorus, a 23-year-old commander in the Prymorsky district, threw his group to the other side, but he was wounded and could not get there himself. I was at the headquarters at the time and heard him reporting. After Redis's strict order, someone rushed after him and pulled him out alive. Khorus, even when he was lying on a stretcher and bleeding after being wounded, gave orders and tried to do everything he could.

The worst thing about all this is not the thought of your death. You can get used to it and even want it to be over as soon as possible. I only wanted it to be quick. We used to joke: why do you need a gun? Hmm, really... I used to be proud of my fancy Stechkin pistol. In the early days of the full-scale war, it was assumed that if you had a Stechkin, you were already Robin Hood. One day, I twirled it in my hands and realized how heavy and uncomfortable it was.

The wildest and most miserable feeling inside is hope, which starts to flicker every time someone hints that you will leave Azovstal.

There are no medicines in Azovstal. There is no anaesthesia, no bandages, no antibiotics, no fresh air, no water, no food. Everything is covered with concrete powder. Operating systems are broken. There are no surgical instruments. There are civilians with children in the plant's nuclear shelters. A person who was in Azovstal understood perfectly well that an injury here means death. With a light wound, there is at least a chance of survival, but a severe one turns into infectious gangrene. Besides, you might not even get to 'Zalizyaka': evacuation groups often came under fire.

People were rotting and dying. Hundreds of wounded doomed to sepsis are delirious. They see and hear someone's leg being cut off without anaesthesia. Someone is drinking antiseptic, running around the bunker with crazy eyes, trying to kill himself. They are lucky if the suicide is at least successful. Some failed, and people were left without a chance for conscious existence.

For several days, Azovstal was buzzing about extradition, a procedure for moving a contingent from enemy-controlled territory to neutral territory. Turkey offered Russia to take us out by sea. There was a proposal to deploy us in Enerhodar, but Putin refused to shut down the Zaporizhzhia Nuclear Power Plant with us.

It was hysteria between complete despair and hope for salvation. Some people began to think it was possible to reach an agreement with the Russians. I somehow started to believe that Turkish ships would come for us, and we would live. The light at the end of the tunnel can also blind you.

It is smart for the enemy to keep us alive. Azovstal has been biting into the ground too hard. When you drive a person into a dead end, they can accidentally show unheard-of strength. The worst thing is that they will later make up myths about it.

The Russians have promised Azovstal defenders an 'honourable captivity' with three meals a day, no bars on the windows, and no physical violence. We must be guarded by the Russian Federal Penitentiary Service. There must be communication with families. Only war criminals will be judged. Our documents, awards, and weapons must be transferred to Ukraine.

We understood that without this, about 600 wounded might not survive. Those who could not stand it morally would surrender but on different terms. We still were waiting for the order. Azovstal can put down its weapons only with a command.

Meanwhile, May was passing. Somewhere far beyond the grey ruins of Azovstal, greenery is visible. When we had a ceasefire, we would climb a tall unbombed building, look into the distance, and talk. It rained and washed away the dust so we could breathe some fresh air. The sun is out, and the sky is as blue as before. The world hasn't changed – only the levels we need to move on change. When you live in such conditions, every level means only one thing: if the previous one is over and you are still here, you always have a chance to pass the next one and survive.

After receiving the command, we handed over our weapons to the main directorate of reconnaissance officer and left Azovstal.

Chapter 5

RING

Oleh Berestovyi is an officer of the Armed Forces of Ukraine, an arthroscopist. In civilian life, he was a top manager in the field of information technology.

Those days, the Russians were convinced that we would kneel down. Well, it happened partially, but there is a caveat.

I asked my friends to find a ring of the right size and bring my girlfriend to me at the checkpoint. I got down on one knee and asked her to marry me.

I might never see her again in my life and really wanted her to have my surname, even if I didn't come back.

In early March 2022, I received an order to go on a mission to semi-sieged Kyiv. I didn't know how the guys and I would get there, let alone how we would return home, or even if we would, come back at all. The course of history was changing every minute. Everything about Kyiv at that time was like a one-way trip.

My beloved would probably want to wear a beautiful dress or something instead of jeans and a sweater at that moment.

'I want to have a child with you.'

'I too want us to have children eventually.'

'You don't get it, I want it now.'

'But I don't know what will happen next. I don't know if I'll be there when you give birth. You may even be left alone with a child.'

'Don't try to convince me. I want to have a child with you right now.'

'Let's make a deal: the desire to have children with you will be my motivation to come back.'

'No. Just now.'

We wanted to become a family. I saw what she was like with kids, and how much they loved her, and I knew she would be a great mom. I also planned to become a father one day. But we had no idea that it could be like this. We were still quite young and wanted a little more time for ourselves to build our family on a stronger foundation. The 25 February 2022 was supposed to be my first day at work as a top manager in a large IT company. Life was gaining momentum, and neither of us was in a hurry.

And what was the point of rushing? I carried her bags in the fourth grade at school and she was in love with me in the sixth grade. Our feelings crossed paths ten years after we last saw each other after graduation. Each of us was married to another person. My beloved lived in the Netherlands for ten years. We were never supposed to meet again, but once, in peacetime, she came to Ukraine to do some paperwork and accidentally settled in a neighbouring street. We met by chance, and then everything happened so she stayed with me in Ukraine.

I put the ring on her finger, and we went to the apartment.

In times of peace, egoism destroys families, while in times of war, it builds them. Lonely people in peaceful cities are not always selfish. But those of us who want to leave a mark in a time of war are always egoists.

When we returned half an hour later, it turned out that the tasks for my group had changed. There was no need to go to Kyiv anymore. On the day of our marriage registration, we took a pregnancy test. Later, in the summer, I went to the front.

I don't know which of us had it harder – me at the front or my wife without me during her first pregnancy. I know that she cried a lot and felt bad not so much because of the explosions and enemy positions nearby, but because she was far away. In the first months of the war, a week feels like a whole month, like Groundhog's Day. Locations were changing, we were changing, but not our days.

But there is something much worse and hurts more than this war. The only thing worse is living out of the context of that.

I sincerely sympathize with the people who did not find themselves in this war and did not feel or touch the paper from which these pages of history were made. They got up but didn't get woken after a missile strike or explosions of kamikaze drones. They did not look for a coffee shop with a generator of electricity in their neighbourhood after massive attacks on infrastructure. They didn't say goodbye to their lovers and greet them with hugs after a long time apart.

When a cluster munition falls somewhere nearby and breaks into small particles, it causes euphoria on a physical level. Not because you realize that this shell cost the enemy several million dollars and you're still alive. This feeling happens literally in the body, and it cannot be reproduced by the mind.

There are things much worse than war.

Worse can only be for someone who wakes up thinking, 'Oh, shit, I have to get up and live through the day again', instead of thinking, 'How wonderful it is that I am alive today.'

I feel sorry for those who have left Ukraine and are stewing in their own guilt over their choices.

I had a friend who recently left for Canada. There is nothing special about this, I'm sure everyone has a friend who left the country during the war. He had wanted to emigrate to Canada for a long time. He entered a Polish university on purpose to be able to cross the border. He spoke emotionally about how he had to fight the system and how unfair this world is. He talked about how he hired lawyers and went to the border with the police. I remember how happy he was when he finally arrived in Poland to continue his journey there. I wanted to be heartily happy for him, but that day an Iskander missile fell nearby, and I didn't have the strength to do so.

Already in Canada, he shared that he would like to give us in Ukraine at least half of the electricity that is available to him. Guilt turns compassion into disgusting pity.

Those who left the country feel guilty towards those who stayed in Ukraine.

Those who walk down the street feel guilty towards those who are sitting in a bomb shelter.

Those who have warmth and light in their homes feel guilty towards those who are freezing and sitting in the dark.

Comrades on the quiet side of the frontline feel guilty towards those in Kherson, Bakhmut, and Soledar.

Those who see enemy positions with binoculars feel embarrassed compared to those who are in captivity.

I came home to work on the point of a permanent location, and I feel guilty because the guys are there now... However, fighting is easier than living in the rear during the war.

When you put on a uniform, it not only gives you a sense of absolute involvement and even safety, but also removes the burden of choice. You don't have to think of anything or decide anything, because you have no options, only orders. The commander will always find a task for you. There is an enemy, there is a weapon, just shoot. In luxury stores, there is always nothing to choose from, people pay dearly for the option of not making a choice.

I wish I believed in God because it would make everything much easier. You always have rules that must be strictly followed. There is always a beautiful mythological explanation for certain things if there is no logic. You can always share the blame if something goes wrong. I tried to believe it many times, but it didn't work out – I'm not used to relying on anyone but myself, and it's not just about responsibility.

Nine months had passed since that hurried March day. Our little son, Theodore, was born. He came into this world not interested in our life plans, but he came to continue life as it was. A real child of war – healthy, screaming loudly, asking for food and changing his diapers, needing attention.

I don't want to leave my wife again, although I am gradually preparing her for it. I don't want to leave my son and return to the cold, mud, and wet roads, but at the same time, I don't want to get off the road because I don't know what to say to my son after such a deed. I want him to be proud of me.

Now he is very small and does not yet realize that I am his dad. But when I take him in my arms, he stops crying. He already knows my scent, and it would be a pity if he forgot it in my absence. I would not want my son to grow up without me at such an important time for him. But I would also not want to miss this breath of the times which we live in. I can feel it blowing at my back. It can be felt on the frontline, in peaceful cities, in destroyed villages, and in those that have already recovered from the occupation. Even in the bomb shelters, where people are no longer afraid, but simply waiting.

This is already everywhere.

Chapter 6

SURVIVE THAT WINTER

Nadiia Mrachkovska is an associate professor of the Department of Finance at the National University of Life and Environmental Sciences of Ukraine, a Ph.D. in Economics, a senior soldier of the 211th Pontoon and Bridge Regiment, and clerk.

'Where are you taking him? You are only wasting time. He's already dead', my neighbour said to me.

I heard him, but I didn't listen. Cherie was still warm. I was horrified and carried him to the twenty-four-hour veterinary clinic in the neighbouring village. Cherie is a Yorkshire Terrier, who is more than a friend to me.

It was still early in the morning and people had not yet left the clinic. The doctor saw my torn jacket and bitten hands and gave me some pills and a glass of water.

'What happened?'

'We were attacked by dogs. They were frightened by today's missiles and attacked me and Cherie.'

'Are you going to leave the dog here?'

'No, I can't!'

'Mrs Nadia, Cherie is dead. Can you hear me?'

'Yes, I hear you.'

'Do you have a place to bury him?'

'Yes, I'll take him to the lake.'

'Do not leave the room until your family gets here.'

'Okay.'

She still unclenched my hands and put Cherie's already cold body in a box and went somewhere. I didn't listen to her, took the box with the dog, and went out to the road.

It was only 9.00 am. It seemed that that road had never seen so many cars in its entire existence as were travelling south of Kyiv on that day, 24 February 2022.

My daughter Ilona came to get me.

'How are you?'

'I'm fine.'

Surprisingly, I was really fine. Just a month before the full-scale invasion began, I had recovered a little after everything that had knocked me down in recent years and I was quite ready. I didn't even cry.

I buried Cherie by the lake. We got into the car and drove away from Kyiv to escape the bombs. This dog was the last point of support for me.

Cherie came to me after my husband left me. He was honest and confessed to me from the bottom of his heart: he had fallen in love. It happens, and I didn't fight for him, no matter what people think. I didn't stop loving my husband and that's probably why I let him go. Everyone has the right to happiness: he has the right to be happy with another person and I must be happy without him. That's how we broke up, although we never officially divorced in our lives.

Perhaps, if Cherie hadn't died that morning, I wouldn't have made the decision to go to the military enlistment office. Such a dog needs care and I'm on duty twelve hours a day – I don't even have time to take myself outdoors.

When I joined the army, we were first housed in a terrible room with no heating – just small, weak electric heaters. Their desperate fight against the cold was a bit like my Cherie trying to fight off aggressive stray dogs.

We slept in sleeping bags, jackets, and hats. I tried not to drink anything at night so that I wouldn't have to get out of my sleeping bag to go to the toilet.

'Oh my God, how to survive that winter?' my colleague said, putting on her hat before going to bed.

I tried to convince her that things are exactly as we think they are.

'We are doing fine. We are needed here and now. We are doing important work. We can see, hear, and breathe. After all, we survived! And our children survived!' I answer her.

Sometimes I remember the first years of Ukraine's independence. Back then, my husband and I, following the birth of our daughter, didn't know how to survive in a penniless environment. We lived in a dormitory and I had no milk for my daughter. My husband used to walk across the park with an aluminium can in the early morning to stand in line to buy milk. To buy a certain kind of baby overalls, we had to wake up at 4.00 am and go to a department store on the left bank of the Dnipro River and stand in a long queue. Sometimes my dad would bring a chicken and a sack of potatoes from the district centre of Pryluky in the neighbouring region. And then I went to work, and my husband continued his postgraduate studies: my salary was about $30, and his scholarship was $4. We lived on that monthly income and even managed to be happy.

'You are so optimistic! I wish we all had that attitude', my colleague said to me instead of saying goodnight. She got a little more inspired and went to bed in her sleeping bag and cold room a little happier than usual.

On New Year's Eve I brought a small Christmas tree into our military office and decorated it with nothing but candy. How much genuine childlike joy we all felt from that tree! How much fun we had!

Perhaps my optimism is not just for me. Or maybe I am just unquestionably happy for the first time in my life. So much that I can share it and be useful in the time and circumstances in which I have to live.

My mother, a native Russian who came to Ukraine to marry my father when she was 18, had long foreseen a terrible war. No one could have convinced her otherwise. However, her sister, who has lived in Tallinn all her life, has always talked about the Crimea annexed by Russia: 'We are not there', 'You are all fascists' and 'You are extremists and Banderites, and you are not raising children properly.' Now that aunt only occasionally asks if my mother is alive on the phone...

I was drafted into the engineering troops of the Pontoon and Bridge Regiment, and here I can really be useful. Of course, no one would send me to the trench – I would be of no use there. But I am good at accounting and public finance, and this knowledge can be the very last drop in the ocean of our struggle against the Russian occupiers. Our soldiers will not fire until they are provided with ammunition, weapons, food, and clothing. And I can make sure that our defenders are not unarmed or hungry with my own efforts and responsibility. This is an interesting, continuous, and responsible job, where I finally felt needed. In science, I didn't feel needed even though I had a significant body of work. I had a ranking, a taste of a life that was not my own, but no sense of the significance of my work and my own integrity. And now I have all this.

My young colleague Arthur from the material service complained that he didn't want a desk job. He was constantly writing reports and trying to transfer to another department.

'Where will you transfer to? You're still so young.'

'What do you mean "where"? All my men are at the front! They have something to tell about the frontline. What about me? What will I tell?'

Arthur was transferred to serve in Kholodnyi Yar after all. He is only 24 years old. I'm not sure if he even realized that hundreds of his comrades depend on his work and that the rear troops are not about sitting in the rear. In our unit there are four combat brigades that go to the frontline to build crossings for logistics in hot spots, and unfortunately, we also have losses, and losses are always indescribably painful.

Have you ever lost someone so badly that a gaping hole appeared in the middle of your chest? Like the one that followed a Russian missile somewhere in Ukrainian Mariupol, Dnipro, Uman or the historic centre of Kyiv?

There is not a single crater in the world – even the one made by a Russian missile – that is not overgrown with flowers or something else. It is filled with life, which is swirling around it – this is just diffusion, and there is nothing you can do about this physical phenomenon.

It was only with the passage of time that I realized I was very sick when my husband left. At that time, I thought my life had come to an end. I cried for two years, but then I looked around me and realized that I suddenly had a lot of time. I can not only teach at the university but also open my own small but cozy business. I can do whatever I want!

In fact, since childhood, I have been obsessed with art and wanted to paint. But my dad said it was madness: artists are lazy, always penniless, and without a crumb in their mouths, and they have neuroses, psychoses, and other misfortunes. You need to get an engineering degree, take an accounting course, go in for biathlon, have money and your own business, and live by the book – and then you will become a human being. I did everything the way my dad wanted.

And then I did what my husband wanted, defended my Ph.D., and started teaching. He didn't like my drawings at first. When we first met, he showed me a photo of himself from the army.

'It's so beautiful! I'll take it and draw a portrait with a graphite pencil – it will be a surprise', I thought, and I took it out and sat over the sheet for a long time before showing him the result.

'What the hell is this?' he said. I was only 23 years old, and his words were, of course, a tragedy. I was very young and could afford to be offended.

When we were no longer together, my daughter gave me paints, brushes, and a certificate to study at an art school. All my life I did what other people expected of me and was unhappy. And then I turned 40 and sat back down at the desk to learn to draw, and I wasn't ashamed.

Now I can take a break from the service on weekends, come to the apartment I rented near my permanent location and enjoy what I love. I have all my paints, easel, and canvases here. Here I can create and think about how to make myself happy in the future.

Every day we have formations, and on Monday we observe a minute of silence for the sons and daughters of Ukraine who laid down their lives for Ukraine. And every time the commander tells us to take off our hats, something inside me rumbles and comes out with tears.

'What's wrong, I'm such a strong woman! Why does this happen every time?' I think when they raise our flag.

But it is at moments like these, when I want to cry, that I realize that nothing can break us. Nothing helps you to understand the need to survive like a maternal instinct. And is there anything more important than to survive?

My dad, who broke me and made me reinvent myself, is no longer alive. I love him so much that I think that's exactly what was needed.

My husband, who broke me later, is no longer alive, but I love him so much that I cannot imagine my life without him – literally. I got very sick with Covid in 2020 and he was the person who took my blood every morning for transfusions after a blood clot. On the day he took me out of the hospital, I didn't recognize myself in the mirror: a spectacularly thin woman turned into a 175 pounds clumsy matron with broken nails after intensive care and boots that wouldn't zip up because of the swelling on her feet.

'We're going to have coffee now.'

'Where am I going to go looking like this?'

'Have you gone mad? I'll bring you everything. Be glad you're alive.'

His death was tragic. Before he died, we even managed to go to his mother's house for the last time and plant currant bushes just as he wanted.

'Why do you need so many currants? What are you going to do with it later?'

'Let there be plenty. Not for me, for us.'

In the last years of his life, before he crashed in the mountains during one of his expeditions, his entire house was covered with my paintings.

And I am happy, just as he said. I feel a strong core inside me. I want to do what I'm good at. I am alive not only from the outside but also from the inside.

Chapter 7

OSELEDETS

Ihor Florko, a fighter of the Azov Battalion, active participant of the Revolution of Dignity. On 20 February 2014, during the Revolution of Dignity in Ukraine, he and his comrades-in-arms (the so-called Angels of Instytutska Street) carried the wounded from under fire. Ihor was 17 years old at the time. Afterward, Ihor graduated from college and fought in the Azov battalion in the east for four years. In 2022, he again went to war against the Russians during a full-scale invasion.

I was walking across the bridge, and a horseman was behind me. He was wearing a black robe with no visible face behind it. Under him, there was a black horse.

I have yet to learn who he is. I don't remember being afraid of him or running away, although at one point I sped up my pace. At the end of that bridge, I looked back and realized that the horseman was not in a hurry. He let me get away.

I rarely have dreams with a strong emotional outburst, but this was exactly the kind of dream. There, I thought that this black horseman will definitely meet me again, it's just a matter of time.

I lived only two years of my conscious life in the civilian world. I started a new life of studying and running my own business. I cut off the Cossack '*oseledets*' that I wore during my service in the Azov Battalion until 2020. With comrades, we wanted to be like real

39

Cossacks and shaved off our heads, except a small piece on the top – the typical hairstyle of a real Ukrainian Cossack.

There is a belief that a Cossack needs this single lock of hair on an otherwise smooth-shaven head to get to Heaven after dying in a fight. When a Cossack dies on the battlefield, an angel takes him by this piece of hair, the '*oseledets*', and pulls him straight to Heaven.

When my mother saw me with such a haircut, she suddenly revealed the secret that it was my natural state. When I was born, I had a completely bald head, with only a long tuft of fine downy hair hanging from the top of my head.

I left Donbas and spent two years of civilian life after my release from the Azov Battalion. That '*oseledets*' meant a lot to me, and I thought that here, in civilian life, I had no moral right to have that on. It was only necessary when I was really in the battles in Donbas.

I believe my dreams. My grandmother Olha has been gone for a long time but she visits me when I sleep. She was a great friend and teacher because she never explained anything. When I was a kid, she told me a lot about the Ukrainian partisans who used to come to her parents, my great-grandparents, at night.

'Grandma, did you see them – those partisans?'

'Yes, but I was just 6 years old, like you, and I didn't understand yet what they were doing.'

'And what were they doing?'

'They were making sure that our country, Ukraine, was independent of the Soviet Union.'

'And they came to your house?'

'Yes. My mom and dad gave them bread and talked to them about different things.'

'And did they visit everyone like that?'

'No, of course, some people did not help them. Although they did not support the Soviet government.'

'And what did they do?'

'Nothing.'

As a child, I was thinking about what it would be like to do nothing and be with no one. Is it possible to do nothing at all and still be someone? Is it possible to be *someone* when you are *with no one*?

I often dreamt that the war was happening again. I was running somewhere through the shelling, trying to do something. These were not pieces of the past. It was a sour taste that appears before you put a lemon in your mouth. The black horseman from my dream caught up with me and I returned to the war.

There was a time in my life when I dreamed a lot about relatives who have long since passed away. They would drag me with them, invite me somewhere. I resisted, but my legs and arms did not obey me, and I could hardly escape from their kindness. During the period when I was dreaming about it, we were having heavy battles, and sometimes I thought that I would soon be dead.

I would wake up tired, as if after hard physical work or when sleeping on a very large bed. When you have your own little corner in which to sleep, you lie down on your side and fall asleep even when it's beastly cold. Sometimes, the guys lie in sleeping bags on the ground, and I used to sleep on the bag of our multiple launch rocket systems (MLRS).[4] You have no room for manoeuvring, no wild boars stomping around you, and no foxes touching your forehead with their wet noses. You have only pure rest. But when you go to sleep in a large bed or on the ground, you have a lot of space, toss and turn, wake up alone – and in the morning it's as if you never slept at all.

Once in a dream, my comrades came and calmed me down a bit. In that dream, there were a dozen of us from Azov, maybe more. They were as happy as *Cossacks Writing a Letter to the Turkish Sultan*.[5]

I wanted to come back to them and be in our Azov fellowship again. And in that dream, we were all waiting for some clerk.

'Guys, I want to come back to you. The clerk will be here soon, tell him that I fought with you before. Let him register me with you.'

'Uh, no, boy, they won't let you. You are definitely not with us.'

41

And the whole team mocked me, laughing like we used to laugh in the basements of the Donetsk region. I was outraged: am I not your equal...? I left home for the Revolution of Dignity in 2013 when I was 17. And have not returned to life yet. Now I'm 27. I still don't know what I'm going to be when I grow up, but I've already eaten gunpowder with you guys...

In the morning, I remembered every face from that dream and thought about every word they said. They didn't want to take me in because none of them were alive anymore. I didn't have a clue who the clerk was, and he never appeared in that dream.

Sometimes I wonder why I'm still here and they aren't.

Although then I saw the clerk again in a dream on the night before Christmas. There were a lot of people in the room, and they surrounded the clerk from all sides. Everyone was trying to talk to him. Everyone wanted to hear the clerk answer their question. Everyone received a piece of truth from him and went away.

I stood to the side and caught his slow and heavy gaze as if he understood all my scepticism about everything that was happening and decided to fight me with his eyes. When there was no one else around, he looked at me and didn't wait for me to come up with a question. 'There is no grave for you on your way, don't overthink', he said, and then I woke up. My heart was still pounding with a frantic force for a long time.

When your comrades die, it seems that death slowly creeps up on you. You learn about the death of a person you don't know. It seems like death is looking in your direction. When you hear that someone you knew had died, it makes a step towards you. And when a fellow soldier dies, it seems that it is already here, about to get to you.

Sometimes guys from Azov come to my dreams alone. Some I knew, some not so much, but I am glad to see each of them. They greet me and say goodbye right away.

'Goodbye. Take care, we'll see you again someday much later.'

I wake up and realize that my comrade from that dream is gone, just like Marcus, whom I met in a dream with another brother-in-arms once again. All three of us hugged each other and sobbed with happiness.

'Holy cow, Marcus, we thought you were dead, but you're alive.'

'Boys, I'm alive, but I still have to go. Bye, take care.'

And he left, smiling, but the other fellow stayed with me in that dream. And in the morning after that dream, I realized that he didn't go with Marcus in that dream, so he must be still alive, although he was in Russian captivity sentenced to life imprisonment.

My comrade Round also came to say goodbye in my dream after the shelling. We were good friends. He was a close friend and deputy of our commander, call sign One-Two. We were supposed to go to dig trenches together, but for some reason, Round went alone, even though he was supposed to take us to that position.

When we all heard about Round's death under fire, we scattered around the dugout to hide our weaknesses in the corners. We didn't want any war or to do any job anymore. A few of us went to that position to take the bodies of our fallen comrades. The shelling continued, and boys dug up Round several times. In the morning, we all went to dig out machine guns, radios, and everything that was covered in the high trenches that we had not yet managed to secure with boards.

The commander, One-Two, was a man of steel. From the first minutes after he learned about the death of his close friend, he continued to hand out decisions in cold blood and show boundless strength: no one get sour, the information is not confirmed, everyone is in place, you are going there, and you are evacuating, etc. We could afford weakness, but he couldn't.

One-Two is now in charge of Azov while Redis is away. He and Round allowed us to come to the command post in the basement when we were standing near Horlivkain in Donetsk region. It was the only place with internet. We could watch videos and listen to

43

how decisions were made in the command. We, ordinary fighters, had much more information than we would have been allowed to know in a regular army.

Sometimes we would work with a mortar and immediately hide in a basement for a long time. There, underground, I shared my thoughts with the guys that we were too used to living together and stopped appreciating what we have here and now.

I suddenly went deep into thought and imagined that I was already very old, and all life was behind me.

I said to the guys, imagine yourself in the future, too. You're sitting by the fireplace, an old fart. You remember your youth and thank God you're alive. And you were born and lived in such a way that just surviving is a miracle. Someday you will look back on these times and wonder how you survived. My friend Ihor Halushka, alias Tesak, while rescuing his comrade Fish from the shelling, received an injury incompatible with life. His left-brain hemisphere was pierced, but he stayed alive and even wins medals in the Invictus Games and continues to serve in the war.

You are an old man. You have a rocking chair, chess, and a bunch of grandchildren. You are bored to death. You have ancient shirts and jackets hanging in your wardrobe that fit you ten years ago. Now you've dried up, and they hang not only in your wardrobe but on you.

You have only a few grey hairs on your head instead of your heavy 'oseledets', and soon the angels will have nothing to pull you to Heaven...

There are no comrades or your brotherhood. There is no possibility to talk to these people with whom you used to have long conversations in basements between shelling, falling down laughing. There is no coffee, no tea ceremonies, and no orange bowl hookah. No shrimp...

Round once told me how he was wandering by the sea when we were standing near Mariupol.

'I saw a net with shrimp', he said, 'and I picked it up. I took it and came to the guys. I said, "Guys, I have shrimps here!" And they were like, "Oh, we just threw out a net too, let's go get them...'"

We laughed like mad, and it will never happen again.

Everything remains in memories.

And people now exist only in memories.

I immersed myself in such thoughts and stewed in all these thoughts for about ten minutes. Then I abruptly came back to reality and was extremely happy that I was still here and with these people. It was like a dream. I told the people around me about my thought experiment. The guys said it was nonsense – only One-Two appreciated the idea.

Then I went to talk to people and bothered everyone, even those with whom I never had anything to talk about. I asked how their day was, how they felt, and what good things happened to them today. In the evening, I thought about how good it was to be here and now.

I squeezed everything I could out of that day.

Chapter 8

PILOT PROJECT

The narrator Andriy Antonenko, call sign Riff, is the front man of the Riffmaster rock band, and an officer in the Armed Forces of Ukraine. In December 2019, he was arrested on suspicion of preparing to murder Ukrainian journalist Pavlo Sheremet. The other two suspects were Yana Dugar, a military medic and an officer in the Armed Forces of Ukraine, and Yulia Kuzmenko, a paediatric surgeon, volunteer, and JFO participant. They were accused of Nazism.

The case appears in social discourse as fabricated with the involvement of the Russian special services. The case sparked a wave of protests across Ukraine.

The charges against Andrii Antonenko: 'Being fascinated by ultranationalist ideas, cultivating the greatness of the Aryan race, dividing society based on nationality, seeking to make his views the object of public attention, while in the [anti-terrorist operation] ATO area, among persons who can handle weapons and explosives, he decided to create an organized criminal group with an aim to murder Pavlo Sheremet.'

When you live on the ground floor, your windows overlook the road, and a bench with old gossip ladies. If you're lucky, you have a view of a flower garden. You have access to a nice but limited landscape. When you move up to the tenth floor, you see not only people but also a park and a lake a mile away. When you want to feel like the master of the world, you leave the tenth floor and go to the mountains. And the further you climb, the harder it is for you.

I joined the Special Operations Forces of Ukraine in 2017, signed a contract, entered the institute, and went to the anti-terrorist operation in Donbas. Everything was according to my plan from raising the barrier to training in the forests and fields, from soldier to sergeant. I would have to start from scratch and I had to give up something on the ground floor to get to the next floor.

'Riff, can't you handle it? You're damn Riff. You're a rock star. Everybody knows you, dude.'

'I cannot. I have to make sure that no one can rub it in my face.'

Then law enforcement came for our souls in December 2019. We were accused of murder, and were to be 'de-Nazified' and 'demilitarized'. Life turned into a black hole. I talked about my case with the guys who came out of surrounded Mariupol.

'They didn't just come for you. A few days later, there was a knock on our door too. It was a wave of arrests, but yours drew all the attention.'

When the war started, I was still under house arrest.

'Svitlana, no one is going to school tomorrow.'

'Why are you panicking?'

'It's not panic, darling. It's not like I work at a poultry farm.'

'What are you going to do?'

'I have no options.'

When the first missile fell somewhere near our house, I fidgeted for a long time and listened to the walls. I have known this sound since 2015. Is it there or not?

I turned on my side. We were lying facing each other. She had both her palms under her head childishly, and her eyes were wide open.

'What are you doing awake?'

'I'm trying to figure out what that was.'

'I see. Wake up the kids and be ready to leave.'

Half an hour after we woke up, a huge black mushroom of haze from Kalibr grew in the neighbouring yard.

In such situations, panic overtakes me later, when all the tasks are completed. My children and wife left the city, and I did not return home after I went to the military base in Brovary town near Kyiv city.

There were ruins all around the shelled base. The building of our unit was shelled. I found a ladder and tried somehow to get to our office on the second floor.

The office survived. Backpacks, helmets, and bulletproof vests in our office were lying neatly where we had put them after we had learned about the departure of the venerable and rich families from Ukraine.

I reached for the pile of bulletproof vests and heard a fighter jet overhead. I gathered all my courage and jumped out the window from a height of 6 metres (20 feet). It seemed to me that I had been flying for a long time.

'Well, I'm not hurt too much', I said to myself. I fell on a pile of bricks.

As it turned out, it was a Ukrainian thing. That was only the first morning of the war in Kyiv and no one understood what was flying over our heads.

Comrades were nowhere to be found. I was supposed to be here with them at night. It was a miracle that the guys didn't get hit that morning. Before the missile came, they went to get weapons together.

'Listen, why are you angry? If you had been here, everything would have been completely different...' said one of them.

If I had been here and not under house arrest, we all might not have survived. All of us.

I had suspected before that our law enforcement officers were working according to the Russians' 'methodology' during my arrest. It became clear why three years ago they came for me, Yana, and Yulia on live TV and put us in handcuffs. We were just a *pilot project*. They needed a big name to make this case public and for the Special Operations Forces (SOF) to lose people's trust. For the military as such to turn into a criminal in the eyes of society. For a volunteer to be an accomplice of a criminal. A soldier was a Nazi, and a volunteer is an accomplice of a Nazi, all of us are nation of Nazis. The enemies' 'methods' have not changed. On 24 February 2022, they came to 'de-Nazify' and 'demilitarize' the whole country and told all the world that they fight Nazis.

We didn't know at that time that Bucha and Irpin, mass torture, mass graves, and reburial would follow. But we, as people wearing military uniforms, knew that we had no right to lie. People were coming up everywhere and grabbing our sleeves like a magic wand.

'Guys, what should we do?'

'Evacuate.'

'Is it *that* bad?'

'It is.'

The people around were making choices every moment, every second. I hate it when I have a choice. I don't know how to make a choice, so I go to my wife, and she does. She is my last resort. When I got arrested, I realized that I did not choose this woman. She is part of the plan for my life, and she is extremely strong.

My wife is my fortress and I have never felt so powerless as when I decided to look into our empty home in early March, between operations.

I came to the apartment and called her. Svitlana was worried and crying. We had moved here just two months before we had to leave our new home. Without her and our children, it was colder at home than it was outside.

'Show me the children's room! And the bedroom! Where's the sofa? And the wardrobe? Oh, we didn't even wash the dishes when we moved out! And who are those people in the flat? Who are they? What are they doing in our house?'

'It's okay', I said, 'they are *ours*.'

My comrades were with me. The coat of arms of the SOF of Ukraine depicts a Seromian wolf. No wonder my wife sometimes resembles Mother Wolf from Rudyard Kipling's *The Jungle Book*. Since my imprisonment, she has developed a new reflex and shows her teeth to anyone who might pose a threat to her family.

When the guys and I left my house, I couldn't pull myself together for a long time. Earlier, during the ATO in Donbas, we knew that they were waiting for us at home. We did not think about whether they were cold or hungry. Then we left home with a light heart and thoughts of returning. And we did return knowing that they were home and safe.

Now, they can be safe anywhere but not at home. They are far away, and no one is waiting for us at home.

My family returned after the Russians surrendered from Kyiv, and it was warm again at home. Things started to live again, and I have somewhere and someone to come back to again. I know that later it will not make such a strong impression and will become routine.

Every person, every thing, every right, and every duty is a part of this big plan, even something trivial. Showering twice a day, fresh bedding, family life and raising kids, education, a spoon for soup, a fork for meat, a fork for fish... Distinguishing one day from another and just leaving the house are also points of this big plan. For some reason, when we settle down somewhere for a long time, we build a toilet first. Our enemies said they come to Ukraine for a long time, and the first thing they did is to tear out the toilet and send it by post to a place where there is no sewage.

I believe that there is a big plan for each of us, not just a pilot project. And it's great if your life plans are part of that big plan. When these things diverge, we call them life exams. If you don't pass this or that exam, something very significant will not happen, there will be no transition to another level. If you don't pass the test, you won't move from the first to the tenth floor. Moreover, you will not have the strength and spirit to go to the mountains.

There must be some reason for which I went to prison and to war. Something for which my children became adults too soon, and for which my wife did not sleep so many nights together.

There had to be something for which the missile arrived twenty minutes after the guys and I had left the location.

There must be something for which all this is going on.

Chapter 9

FLOWERS FOR MOM

Bohdan Runic, call sign Runa, is a former fighter of the Azov unit. The interview with Bohdan took place in June 2015 at the Azov base. In 2014–2015, he participated in the anti-terrorist operation in the east of Ukraine. At that time, Bohdan was a 19-year-old student of the National Tax Academy of Ukraine. Back in 2015, Bohdan assumed that the war would unfold not only in the east, but also in other parts of Ukraine.

My parents lived through Ilovaisk and turned grey. I mean, they have never physically been to this town, but I, their son, was there.

They usually guess everything about me, although I keep a lot of things to myself. Before the battles, I still call and say that I'm fine and I will have scheduled training. So, the connection may be low. Thank you (adding 'for everything' but only in my mind). Goodbye. See you soon. I promise to call you tomorrow. Everything is fine. Goodbye once again. If not, then I lost my phone, or the battery is dead and there are no other options. (In fact, I always have two more batteries.) Finally, goodbye.

I used to say this even before the difficult storming of Mariupol when we entered Starobeshevo. But I stopped promising to call tomorrow there, in Ilovaisk when I realized that there were practically no chances.

Mom and Dad had already given up arguing: 'How could you go there without our permission? What do you do this for? We brought you up, and you spit on us…' In such cases, I always think that when you have grown even an indoor flower, you shouldn't put too much hope in it. Even indoor flowers will wither away one day and break your hopes.

They say I'm going nowhere. But what do you mean going nowhere? If I don't do this, then very soon the war will be somewhere in Mykolaiv or Dnipropetrovsk region. And even in this case, our state will provide weapons only when the enemies are already somewhere in the forests of the Kyiv region.

I know only that either you support me, and I do as I know. Or you don't support me, but I still do as I see fit. Of course, you gave birth to me and put me on my feet, but I must go on my own. And my choice will not depend on whether you give me, a poor student, some money for a bulletproof vest and a helmet...

Or the typical parental what-will-happen-to-us-if-you-die issue. I say, there are some people who came to work in the Twin Towers in New York on time on 9/11. And there are those who did not because of the flu, for instance. There are people who were born between 1939 and 1945, and there are those who died. There are always people who did not make it to the flight when the plane crashed. Billions of people on the planet don't like carrot juice, and one British man named Basil Brown loved it so much that he drank a lethal dose of 38 litres (10 gallons) in a week.

You can go to a volleyball game, suddenly stumble, and become crippled. Or you can come back from the war as a completely healthy and fulfilled person.

Although how can you feel fulfilled when you must bring proof to the dean's office stating that you were absent from the university because you were in the trenches and got out of encirclement? I had to have a serious conversation for my studies not to be interrupted. I said, if you guys in cabinets accept this state of affairs, it would be nice of you, thanks. If not, I will just write an application for expulsion from the university.

When I'm not on duty, I still go to lectures. I take exams, negotiate with professors about everything. They say I am a dark horse. My classmates are convinced that I am a freeloader. They cram everything until they pass out, while our Parliament is literally tearing our tax legislation to shreds: everything you said yesterday at the exam is no longer relevant today.

But that's not the point. If I hadn't been allowed to stay at the academy, I would have piled up books and swallowed them with no hope of getting any marks. And I'm sure that I would have done much better in life than a lot of the excellent students. It's not vanity, it's how things work.

However, immediately after my exams at the academy, I was asked to teach new recruits at our unit and to conduct tactical classes. I'm a fresh-baked junior sergeant in an assault company and act as an instructor at the training centre. So fresh, that in the first week of my practice, an older man, who had served in the armed forces, stared at me with the look of someone who thought he had entered the wrong door. He was being taught about how to keep the defence on the eastern borders of his homeland by a 19-year-old boy whose voice changed yesterday.

But after two weeks I met him at the frontline. It was very nice to hear words of gratitude and recognition from an older man. I guess age doesn't mean anything. I have my own special division of people. Some talk a lot, but they are permanently disorganized, disoriented, and undisciplined while working. Others talk a little (and maybe that's why!), but do everything clearly, although not always by the rules. During training, we consider various options, but none of them is realized in real combat. Everything requires an individual approach if you are doing it not for self-assertion, but for results.

This war can be compared to the First World War: positional battles, artillery, tanks, meat, etc. Sometimes elite units are sent by their superiors into ambushes. I'm prone to think that civilians should be annoyed by all this in the first place. They shouldn't forgive such things and give up and irresponsibly say 'I don't read the news or watch TV'. I mean if they want to live in a civilized world. The desire to claim rights and not fulfil any responsibilities has nothing in common with civility.

Of course, war is not about human civility at all, but civility is essential in war. And it is not in medals and awards. When you are given a piece of metal instead of documents and guarantees after you hit a tank on the frontline, you have no choice but to put it in a prominent place at home and be proud of yourself, especially if you have no reason to go out. Yes, maybe it was thanks to you that some tank did not reach Kyiv, but so what? You don't have money for the subway…

We really lack military therapists and specialized psychological assistance centres. In fact, in a country at war, such places should be everywhere. When you get off the public transport, you should be able to ask passersby, 'Where is it in this neighbourhood?' as if asking about the nearest bank branch.

To be honest, I don't believe that the folk can stop it. I don't believe in the folk at all. Humans are just humans. Yes, they strive for good things like family prosperity, raising a child, planting a tree, going to work every day, and other good things. But in Donbas, I also saw people who had been living with Soviet passports for decades of Ukrainian independence, not realizing that they were already living in another country. Or those who are nostalgic for cheap sausage. Those who are nobody without some others who take a decision instead of themselves.

Folk is just a form, not a content. Content is a nation.

To become a nation, one must be independent in everything. One must get off your parents' backs. One should buy themselves a helmet and bulletproof vest. One should graduate from university or something.

I want to continue studying because I really need to get off my parents' back and bring something to the family. This meagre scholarship allows me to make a minimal gift to my family once a month. To buy flowers for Mom, for example.

I have something to say to the idiots who ask me what I will do when the war is over. I don't know if I will live to see it. (Some guys from the 93rd Mechanized Brigade captured a Russian officer at the Donetsk airport and asked him why the war was taking so long. He just laughed: 'Haven't you realized anything yet? To crush the youngsters and the infrastructure.')

But it will end, I know. The only question is when.

Chapter 10

MIRROR

The narrator of this story is Yaryna Chornohuz, a Ukrainian poet, military medic, and intelligence officer of the Armed Forces of Ukraine.

War as a form of human activity demeans the human species. It turns out the best inside features of a person, like courage, honesty, and endurance – but it literally turns out one's insides. In war, people go missing. But even in war, sometimes they only begin to be human. War rips a person from their family and rips off their legs…

It shows that we all have the same blood flowing inside us. War shows blood too much. I hate the smell of it, so thick, sweet, and sickening, like the enemy's smile.

War does humiliating things to the human body. No matter how inspired the human spirit can be in the battle, the body can leave these cold lands mutilated. Or not leave… Remarkable deeds exist only in the war movies, where a character pulls the body of a fallen comrade out from under fire. This is a unique luxury. Retrieving a body from the battlefield can cost several more lives.

I wanted to feel the battle. Before the full-scale Russian invasion, we with our comrades had been stewing in our own juices for a long time, moving to villages north of Mariupol from the Luhansk oblast. We planned to stay there to dig shelters, take turns, and work on Russian convoys with NLAWs (missle system)[6] near Novoaydar.

We were ordered to move. Our company of the 140th Battalion was reinforcing the 36th Marine Brigade in the villages northern to Mariupol. We arrived in Rozivka village on 27 February when the Russians were already capturing Nikolske village. The five of us slept in our BRDM (combat reconnaissance patrol vehicle) like in a tin can. I did my best to wrap my legs, but it was so cold there that I couldn't get warm.

On 4 March, the five of us were at an observation post on the road from Vyshnuvate village. The village had already been captured by the Russians. We were supposed to report if we noticed Russian vehicles, and then quickly retreat to another village and join the general defence.

In the morning, we warmed up our tea and got ready to have breakfast.

'Look, something is coming', one of us said.

We left our dry rations and took out our binoculars. I lifted my drone into the sky. On one side of our observation post was a field, and on the other side was a forest. A huge Russian column was moving towards us.

We reported to our commands.

'It's our guys who got out of the encirclement. Go for interaction', they said.

One of the greatest officer phobias in the early days of the war was 'friendly fire'. The commanders were afraid of shooting between their people.

Two of us went forwards, but with weapons prepared. The tank in front of us started to point its turret at those guys, and then abruptly turned its attention to our BRDM, where Ivan, the gunner, was sitting. I was standing next to it.

The fire was coming at us from every kind of weapon we could imagine at the time. Our fire in response did not help to hit the enemy as much as it kept our consciousness in good shape after a fresh contusion.

'I flew out of that BRDM like a champagne cork', the gunner Ivan said later when we came to the general defence in the village. Ivan almost had his leg and arm amputated. He was lucky enough to see the tank's turret while he was inside. The shell was not a high-explosive, but an armour-piercing one, which penetrates armour and sets vehicles on fire.

No one thought we would survive. I think it was probably how people looked at Jesus Christ when he came out of the tomb after moving the 500-kilogram (1,000-pound) stone and came to Galilee.

Not that I am a very devout Christian. My baptism happened after a sniper's bullet stopped the life of my then-boyfriend Mykola, alias Red, in 2020 in Donetsk region. We had just started our relationship and it was filled with the kind and sincere things that happen between people in the first months of dating. During his funeral service, I decided to be baptized, although I do not believe in the catechism. My faith is more mystical.

Just in a week near Mariupol, we shot all the ammunition we had and were almost naked and barefoot. We saved the wounded but could not afford to take the bodies of the dead. We were ordered to withdraw and save what we had. Somebody had to hold the next village. Russian troops would go on, stepping over the bodies of our comrades. The bodies of those who were begging to be shot because they had lost their legs and arms and did not want to live anymore.

I was supposed to go on a mission with the reconnaissance group, but I was left behind just in case a paramedic was needed. They completed the task, found positions, drew maps, stopped to smoke, and were about to move back when suddenly a mine exploded nearby. We came running from the observation post and found three dead people and one seriously injured by debris.

We were driving for a long time – forty minutes at least. On the way to the hospital, this guy was coughing up blood. At the hospital, he was still conscious. The next day, they told me that the debris got between the hemispheres of the brain. This was the first time they had ever failed to stabilize a wounded man.

He died there, in the hospital, and it was something incomprehensible to me. Just how? We had come too far, too hard. That's not how people do things... he should have survived.

And yes, the Russians would go further, even though the idea of a full-scale war seemed like a fairy tale to many Ukrainians. They were shocked on the morning of 24 February, not noticing the nearly 13,000 people who died in the war for Ukrainian Crimean Peninsula and Donbas over the past eight years. Even after the first missile strike, they began to expect the good tidings of a quick and safe end to the war. I don't see a big difference between the Russians who wanted to take Kyiv in three days and the Ukrainians who expected the war to end in two or three weeks.

Waiting for good tidings, like hoping for a good king, is an ancient imperial relic. You could disbelieve in the Russian invasion as much as you wanted, but in 2014, they already occupied Ukrainian Crimea, Donetsk, and Luhansk, so it is natural that they will go further.

The Russians have been shooting and deporting us throughout the century, so it is natural that they will go further.

The Russians have not allowed us to speak Ukrainian at home for several centuries, so it is natural that they will go further.

The Russians burned down the Zaporozhian Sich[7]. It is natural that they will go further.

The Russians have been preparing all the time since Ukraine regained its independence, so it is natural that they will go further.

Our reconnaissance group commander Perun[8] knew not only that there would be a big war. He also knew his fate. He said that if he was going to die, it would be in battle with the enemy. While we were looking for shelter under bombardments, he covered us. Perun ran out to the elevator, hit a Russian tank with the NLAW, and then fell himself.

How much I adored him... he was professional, strong, fair, and creative. He wrote amazing songs about the war and sang them while playing his own guitar.

It was he who taught us how to walk in the grey zone. In the summer of 2021, Perun took me to patrol the island of Dzharylgach[9] to see if I could walk 10 kilometres (6 miles) in the heat of the day across the largest uninhabited island in Europe with a medical backpack and equipment. And I did it!

Perun was very fond of nature and rejoiced like a small child when he found a deer antler on the island. He was the only one who wasn't afraid when we all heard a growl in the dark somewhere in the forest, and then saw a wolf in the thermal imager. He said the wolf was smart and would never attack a superior force. We gathered the courage, lined up in a chain, and calmly walked around the beast.

Perun hated crying for those killed in battle. While we were on rotation for eight months before the full-scale war, he asked us not to cry for him when he was gone. When you can't believe that such people can exist, you can't believe that they can die. A machine gun bullet hit the side of his body armour. Senior Lieutenant Anton Hevak, our Perun, the commander with whom we were ready to go into battle, died on the way to the hospital on 5 March 2022. He was 27 years old.

War has been misconstrued and defiled by culture. Death in battle is supposedly heroic and beautiful. It is fully consistent with the choice of a person who went to the battlefield and returned on a shield. Like it has a sacred purpose. But it is trivial, always unfair and humiliating, especially to the one who questioned it. If you don't want to accept the reality around you and die peacefully on the toilet or in bed at 95, then die young in battle...

Not afraid to die in battle? Live on in legends...

Want to become a legend? Then let no one ever know if you are alive.

Russians have a lot in common with death itself. They mock the bodies of those who are not afraid of them most desperately.

When we were retreating from the village of Zachativka near Mariupol, Russian tanks were destroying home after home in that village. We had nothing to respond with. Five minutes into the fight – three were wounded. With one hand, I was putting tampons on Achilles's cheek. I even thought, thank the Lord that a fellow with such an alias didn't get wounded in the heel... With another hand, I was tightening the harness around someone else's trousers. Blood from his shrapnel wound was seeping through his trousers. I was screaming to everyone to run for cover, and through my own screaming, I heard somebody say that Curl was shot.

Curl was the call sign of my husband, and we were only just starting out our marriage. We could not be together for two years while we served in different units. Finally married officially, we spent only ten days together and then had to separate again: I headed south, and he headed to Donbas. We reunited again only when he came to our joint position on 22 February. He shook the hand of our commander, got his grenade launcher, and stayed with me.

Someone with a beard fell face down at our positions. I ran to help him as other wounded approached our positions. I turned the soldier's body over. It was the commander of another unit, Hector. He had a head wound.

My husband ran up to me immediately when the Russians started to advance in unison, like a single wall. Such advances always happen after the heavy bombing. I got the stretcher ready for Hector.

'No, we are leaving', I heard. Only a handful of ours was left. Our commander ordered us to retreat. This is not how a blockbuster about our future victory should look. This is not how heroes should appear.

Hector was cramping in agony. All I had time for was to cover him with a blanket in the hope that stray dogs wouldn't eat him. We thought this advance would stop and we could come back to get him, but we were not able to retrieve many of our men.

I don't know what was harder: talking to Hector's parents or coming to terms myself that he is no longer here. To answer all this, I need to find an answer for myself first.

I heard his agonizing breath; I saw how he clenched his teeth and went blue. He was already staring into the abyss and did not hear anything around him. Yet sometimes I still think he may be alive. There are photos of a boy who is a prisoner of war and who is alive. Sometimes I dream about him. I was advised to talk to him in my thoughts – that he would hear me if he was alive, regardless of the thousands of miles between us.

I sometimes ask myself all these questions. What happened to Hector? How could it be that Perun knew beforehand how his life would end? What is the sense in Achilles's dying after surviving that cheek wound near Zachativka village? Why did that recce fighter, whom we carried for so long to the hospital, die? Why wouldn't Red wait for the full-scale invasion to start?

Why did Violinist die?

Why Amazon?

Why Daisy?

But it's not these 'why' questions that need answers. These questions only put a mirror in front of you.

Look closely.

You will never find answers to all these questions in that mirror. But you will get something else that helps you find the strength within yourself to move forward.

Chapter 11

GRANDPA

Denys Kobzin is the director of the Kharkiv Institute for Social Research and a human rights activist. Denys dedicated his work to fighting torture in law enforcement. He took part in combat operations as a member of the Kraken unit and the 112th Brigade. Here, he talks about the most challenging combat experience of his life, which took place during the defence of the Kharkiv region in April 2022.

I climbed the fence and fired my assault rifle.

'Guys', I said, 'Give me something else. That one jammed.'

The boys gave me someone else's machine gun. I shot, but it didn't work either. This has never happened to me before.

'Grandpa, maybe you should do it; you're a hunter.'

'I'm not going to do that.'

In almost every unit, there is a man who chooses the call sign because he is the eldest one in the group. Just like in every military unit of the Ukrainian army, there is a guy called Beard because he is bearded: in my unit, it is me.

Grandpa is the only person from our group whom I knew during that operation of clearing the village of Ruska Lozova. Russians drove back there when they were trying to break through to Kharkiv. We had to inspect the territory, help the civilians, and 'cleanse' the village of occupiers in case they were hiding somewhere in the basements.

The scout gave me his AR. It had so many additional devices on it that I got confused, pointed it a little to the side of the target, and missed it for the third time. The 'target' got scared and ran somewhere behind the vast, red-roofed house we were trying to get into.

A man came out of the house with his hands up.

'Don't shoot! There are children in the house.'

The only child in the house was this huge white alabai dog who did not let us inside to set up observation posts. I could see in his playful and silly eyes that this dog could not be more than 1 year old. I was the only one who volunteered to shoot him. There is no frontline: there can be both our own and occupants everywhere; it is dangerous to be on the street with a group of armed men.

When we had just settled in the house, heavy shelling from both sides started: artillery, tanks, mines, grenades, and phosphorus. The house was shaking so much that even I was surprised, and it was hard to surprise Kharkiv residents at that time with shelling. During the first months of the full-scale invasion, we in Kharkiv did not count the 'calibres' above our heads. Kharkiv was their idea of a fix while they were crossing other regional centres to get to their dream, Kyiv, as quickly as possible.

One day in Kharkiv, I woke up with an incomprehensible feeling and tried to understand what had happened in my dream. There had been no shelling for an hour between 5.00 and 6.00 am. I suddenly recognized birds singing. The silence was so thick that it was almost deafening.

All was quiet around the house with the red roof. Everything was burning and smouldering. Grandpa and I waited there and returned to the church. The Russians knew that the church was the headquarters, and it was also on fire. However, there was no one there anymore: civilians with Easter cakes and candles ran to the basements, and the military went to clear the village.

Grandpa and I met a company commander.

'Who's with the grenade launcher? There is a danger of a breakthrough; we need grenade launchers.'

'I have a grenade launcher!' Grandpa, a fan of weapons, immediately responded. But he also realized what he had done. A grenade launcher never bodes well. Grandpa is far from being a young man clinging onto life, but he is not old enough to not hold on at all.

There was something in Grandpa's sad eyes that pulled me with an invisible thread. We were put on a bus and taken to the edge of the village. On the way, they picked up about a dozen men like Grandpa. It was evident that they had difficulty wearing body armour. Some very young boys looked like yesterday's schoolchildren. The faces of these young men shone with anticipation of adventure. The only difference between old and young was their eyes, searching for something and radiating expectations of the first battle in their lives.

One of those teenagers from yesterday sat down with me.

'Hey, Pops, will you be my number two? I'm Chief.'

Chief looked to be no more than 20, and he was really like a son to me. Then another boy approached Grandpa and me, asked to join us, and told us about Chief.

'Guys, can I stick together with you on duty?'

'Are you mad? We have the most dangerous place here.'

'But I'll have to stand guard with someone anyway. You're the sanest of all of us here, and Chief and I were on training a week ago.'

From the first day, I had been feeling unrealistic about everything that was happening around me. How do you contain this breakthrough? With Kalashnikovs and small-calibre mortars? We were promised ammunition, but now we don't have it. There is no food or water. We must get food in abandoned houses and drink water with cigarette butts at the bottom of rusty buckets. We must fight side by side with people we have never met before. Each new junction left behind more questions than we brought with us.

One day, while on duty, Grandpa and I were looking at the warm, red sunset and talking about everything until a fierce shelling started that blew a piece of the wall off.

'Grandpa, are you okay?'

'I'm fine, they just put out my candle, the bastards!'

I shone my flashlight at Grandpa. He was holding his fist with a piece of candle in front of him. The fragment cut it in half at the level of Grandpa's hand. A millimetre lower and Grandpa would have bled.

Grandpa and I were thrilled that we had to stay here until the morning: the National Guard would soon arrive and replace us. This meant that we could step back and breathe a little.

Grandpa and I took turns and went down to the basement to nap. Several people were already on the floor, and near them were two old dogs: a corgi and a shepherd. No one paid attention to us except the dogs, who pierced us with pitiful looks and begged us not to throw them out. For the first time in a few days, we closed our eyelids, but suddenly someone ran into our sleepy realm: we were under attack.

We jumped out of that basement under machine-gun fire with bullets ricocheting one after another. Everyone was scattered, who knows where.

'Who knows how to shoot a sniper rifle?'

'Me!' Chief was shouting. I'm sure he had never held a sniper rifle in his hands before. Chief looked around and caught my eye.

'Cover me!' he shouted to me.

We ran to find a place to shoot from. We could have gone into an abandoned house, but Chief and I had nothing to break down the door with. Suddenly, right next to us, the Russians hit a house. It crashed inside with a loud bang and turned the house into a pile of bricks.

'Chief', I shouted, 'stop shooting! Because we are next.'

Chief was running to different corners looking for a place to shoot, and I was setting him up. And so, it happened – I became this guy's number two. It was likely his first fight, and I wanted to see Chief survive.

When the assault was repelled, I looked around once again. Where were all the people I came here with? And most importantly, where was Grandpa? I asked almost everyone I met about it. No one had seen him.

I went to the checkpoint with another group of new people, and there we were shelled so hard that I started to pray. If I didn't believe in God, I would probably have learned some existing prayers for such an event. But I did believe in something; I didn't know the canonical texts, and I came up with combinations of words that seemed to me to be similar to prayer.

I was in the same dugout with some accidental guy. Cassette after cassette was laid down, mine after mine. My neighbour was very sick, and I tried to constantly give him simple tasks and draw his attention to the world around him so that he wouldn't be completely overwhelmed. It helped me to also keep my grip on reality.

At one point, I felt completely at ease. I didn't do anything intentionally, but it was as if I saw myself from the side.

I saw myself jumping up and down from the shock wave, although I hardly felt it physically. I saw the involuntary horror on my face at what was happening here and now – and also the quiet sadness at what was happening at all.

I noticed that my lower lip was bloody. The skin was dehydrated and cracked after three days of no food and sleep.

I saw myself lying there with the machine gun, waiting for it to end.

The feeling of control that the machine gun gives you is illusory. Here the war has started. Here you have stood in a mile-long queue behind it. Now it is in your hands, and the enemy is on the ring road of your city. Now you see someone who has come to shoot at you. You shoot first... no, it rarely works that way. In this war, there are very few situations where an assault rifle saves you. Usually, you don't see the enemy – the walls in front of you, the sky, and the forest are shooting at you, but not the person.

I saw myself who missed my family very much. I wondered how my family was doing. My wife and son didn't leave Kharkiv and stayed to help the old and infirm under the shelling. All this time, it was as if we were all in the same city but very far away from each other, sometimes unable to exchange messages about our safety and health.

I realized that I had been all alone for many days. There are a lot of strangers around me. All I have is Grandpa. But where is he now? What happened to him?

I saw myself from the outside, and perhaps that saved me. It seemed that if I had been hit, it wouldn't have hurt as much because I was no longer there – not in my own body. I would look at myself bleeding, but it wouldn't hurt.

During this shelling, the last cassette hit a neighbouring dugout, and a bloody company officer was pulled out. He got some shrapnel under his body armour. He was a giant man weighing about 130 kilograms (290 pounds). We had to walk about 0.5 kilometre (a third of a mile) to the nearest evacuation point. We put him on some doors and just pulled him while he was rolling from side to side and wheezing from a pneumothorax. It was impossible to put him in the evac, so we put him half alive in the back seat.

There was no point in returning to that checkpoint – almost nothing was left of it. I went down to some basement. People – as always, those I see for the first time in my life – opened cans of compotes and cucumbers that they found in the basement, drank and chewed something. I bandaged a guy and fed another guy some caramels. His heart was breaking at the sight of the dying company man. He needed Validol, but no one had it. I gave him two sweets, and the increase in blood sugar made him feel better.

We ran to the evacuation point under mortar fire, dodging between the houses so the Russians could not see us from their helicopters. People were exhausted and running hard. Some of them were elderly or out of shape.

When I got to the evacuation point with all those people, the Russians had poured several drone strikes there. We sat down to wait for the evacuation, smoked, and experienced the acute euphoria of surviving. Some guy noticed me looking at the water bottle in his hands and gave it to me. I greedily swallowed everything in it, even though there was more saliva in that bottle than water. Only then did I realize how thirsty I was.

They took absolutely everyone; only no one came for me. I called my relative, and he came to pick me up in a civilian car.

I didn't meet Grandpa.

Chapter 12

COMMANDER

The narrator is Lesya Shemberko, commander of a military assault platoon of the 128th Separate Mountain Assault Brigade. She participated in the defence of Ukraine on the southern front in 2022.

I was sitting on the metal armour of a combat vehicle and looking at the sky. My fingers and toes were numb. The cold air stroked my face like a dangerous razor. My white nails were glowing in the dark: I had planned a holiday in Cyprus the day before and had had my nails done.

We marched towards Melitopol on 25 February 2022. There are still a lot of us. Neither the beginning nor the end of our column is visible.

Our vehicles are in terrible condition. It seemed that if we got from point A to point B, for these tin cans, it would be a feat. But only we knew about it – for Russian aviation, our combat vehicles are still targets. We had to be cautious in case something other than frozen rain started falling from the sky.

Suddenly, our driver fell asleep while driving, and it slid into a ditch. People scattered to the four corners of the globe. While falling, I reflexively reached for my radio and assault rifle and then allocated everyone onto other combat vehicles. I sat down on a random tank and stuck my icy feet into the open hatch. Warm air was barely coming out of the hatch. In a few hours, we reached Vasylivka in Zaporizhzhya region, where I was able to sleep for an hour or two. My group was left in reserve.

The war is rushing from everywhere, and there is no longer a home front. It is not clear which villages are occupied. When tanks drove by, I fell to the ground with everyone else and was afraid to raise my head. I thought that as soon as I looked in the direction of the vehicles and saw a person, eye contact would instantly happen. There is a certain illusion that people don't see you until you look at them. And if there were enemy tanks that passed by, you automatically found yourself behind enemy lines.

In Vasylivka, we were given an ancient Ural truck, which we used to drive to the town of Tokmak. It was only 5.00 am, but locals were wandering on the streets. Some kind people brought us tea to warm up, and duct tape for me: my trousers were torn, and it was the only way to save me from the cold. People were curious how we got there at all. There were a lot of broken Ukrainian vehicles around.

'There is a Russian checkpoint near the road to Orikhiv…'

'This is impossible, we were travelling in a convoy in the morning, and it was empty.'

'But they pushed us face-first into the ground! Russians are already there.'

Somewhere nearby, we heard a machine gun fire, and we started to get out of there almost by touch, as there was no internet or maps.

One of the locals recommended a road near the cemetery, and it didn't take long to get there. We saw a vehicle with the letter Z and started to turn right around. I thought we were done for. It would have been faster to ride a snail and get out of there than to drive our Ural. The Russian tanks were breathing down our necks for a long time. I don't know who was praying for us then, but there was not a single shot fired at our side.

We came back alive from the cemetery, and townspeople greeted our Ural with surprised eyes. The town was already teeming with Russians. I don't even remember which road we took to get out of the centre of town. But I quickly came to my senses when someone shouted 'Medic! Medic!' That was the first time I saw a man's body mutilated by the war – with bloody, broken, and twisted limbs. It was Valichka, the 20-year-old paramedic from our unit. After that, she stayed in a coma for more than a week and underwent rehabilitation for several months.

People in the villages where we stopped for defence were afraid to help us. Some man brought us a pack of boiled eggs and a bowl of pasta. We had no food, so we happily peeled the eggs for our people on the first line of defence. However, the man who came to us with the food did not have enthusiasm at his glance.

'I will do everything for you I can, but don't come to my house. We don't know what will happen next, and I still have to live here', he said to us.

The village where we stayed was called Myrne. The villagers laid a cable for us to the beekeeper's house so that we could have electricity.

'Do you have a wife or daughter?' I asked a local when he handed me a pair of warm sweatpants and a sleeveless shirt. He recoiled, but then quickly got what I meant.

All my things were left in that combat vehicle in the ditch. The man's wife and daughter brought me pads and new underwear of my size. I held it all, and my hands were shaking. Things happening around me erased from my memory not only fresh underwear as it is, but also the fact that I was a woman and would have my period. Later, we put women's pads in our boots to keep our feet from getting wet, but it only helped for a short time, and made the shoes with mud on the soles even heavier.

People never stopped offering us help.

'Have you eaten anything?'

'No, we only have dry rations.'

'But I heard somebody cooks for you there.'

'We don't know about that, we have almost nothing.'

'Wait. And come to my house to wash in turn.'

I forced my boys to wash. Taking a shower in that situation seemed like a miracle. They refused and sent me first. For the first time in my life, I was having a shower with a radio by my side.

Soon afterwards, a drone flew into our square. Someone gave the order to neutralize it, and twenty minutes later mortar fire began. The village lost electricity, the internet, and water. It was being shelled from all sides, and in the morning on the fourth day, we withdrew from Myrne village to the neighbouring village, Shcherbaky, on the second line of defence. While we were smoking with our mortar battery commander on the porch of an abandoned house, mortar fire started. The sound was getting closer and closer. It seemed that soon our cigarettes would not be lit by lighters.

'Is it for us?'

'Yes, just a little closer.'

'And that one…?'

'Even closer…'

Then everything exploded, literally in a second.

'Now we must run as fast as we can!', my friend said.

The mortar fell in front of the gate, a few metres from the house where we had been smoking on the porch.

'Well, kid, do you like this war?'

'Nah… not very interesting or pleasant.'

Many wounded and killed were brought from the neighbouring village on the first line of defence. People were tired and giving up. We had at most two minutes to take a defensive position. I had to choose my words like never before in my life to make them keep going, and I had very little time for that. It was like a balloon: if you touched it wrong, it would explode.

I was looking for people to crew a combat vehicle and did not find anyone. The minimum crew of an infantry fighting vehicle is three people: a commander, a gunner, and a driver-mechanic.

It was exploding over the horizon; people were exploding too. One of our old men was suitable for the driver-mechanic – a silent, kind man, less than a year away from retirement. He had been turning nuts all his life.

'Grandpa, you should get in the car, please...'

'No, your cars live for twenty minutes at most.'

'Please, Grandpa, pull yourself together. Here's a cigarette. Let's smoke together and think about everything. I even found a gunner.'

'Do whatever you want with me. Let it be a crime or jail or whatever, but I won't go there.'

I lied to him: there was no gunner. The brigade commander did not want to hear it.

'Look for the gunner!'

'There was none. There were grenade launchers and shooters, but no gunners.'

'Do whatever you want! Just give birth, anything... we need a gunner.'

But even when I found people for the crew, it didn't help. The Russians went straight for our battalion headquarters. Our commander was killed. Women were being taken out of the village, but I did not go to the evacuation. My male comrades and I left the besieged village on foot through the forest and fields.

Many died. There was nothing to fight with. Weapons seemed like a heavy burden. People didn't understand the point of carrying a machine gun if a tank or helicopter can start shooting at you at any second from anywhere.

When we were walking during the day, it was very hot and unbearably difficult to carry ourselves with our wet clothes. My feet would get stuck in the mud. The old man, the mechanic who I was campaigning to join the crew of the combat vehicle, was walking with us. He had problems with his feet, and his calluses were as big as my fists.

I threw my gloves and warm vest aside somewhere along the way. Only in the evening did I find out what a terrible mistake I had made. It was getting colder and colder, and we had neither sleeping bags nor mats.

Late in the evening, it became clear that we had no strength to go on, so we went to sleep in a forest. I was shivering from the cold. Last year's dry grass, which we had gathered nearby to somehow cover ourselves, did not help. We couldn't make a fire – something was constantly flying overhead. The Russians knew we were in that forest: a crowd of fifty people is hard to miss.

I don't know if we believed then that we would reach somewhere and survive. I believe in God but didn't want to pray. I think that if we had started talking and thinking about whether we believed in this or that, we would not have escaped.

'Max', I said to my comrade-in-arms, who was walking beside me, 'Do you know what I want now?'

'What, Lesya?'

'Varenyks! Small ones, with thin dough.'

'With what filling?'

'With cherries! Sour ones, but with sugar. So that they melt in your mouth and pinch your tongue.'

'Sounds like a plan…'

Of course, we had no food. There were almost no cigarettes left.

My husband really doesn't like smoking. He didn't like this past habit of mine, although, on the most difficult days, he would pass me cigarettes when I asked.

After my group and I barely escaped the encirclement, we were rehabilitated for about a week, and a few days later we were sent back to our positions to hold the line.

Once in Zaporizhzhia, I met a local from the village of Myrne, where we were standing. He told me that after us, about 200 military machines and a lot of Dagestanis entered the village. Our job was to be a manoeuvrable defence. We had to juggle with fire for a short time so that everything didn't burn down at once, and so that they had time to set up defensive positions behind us.

I found out that I was pregnant when I decided to take a test at the pharmacy during the delay, just in case. I had already resigned from my position as a unit commander and was suffering a lot because of leaving my people and stopping to do what I had been working towards for so long.

I could not fulfil my duties and blamed myself for being pregnant at such a time. I could neither work in the war, nor bear a child under fire.

When I arrived in Kyiv after demobilization and stepped onto the platform, my tears poured out. Life must be completely different now.

I was responsible for the department, but it was easier than being responsible for the person inside me.

I could ask my husband on the radio how he was doing and understood everything from the sounds around him. It was much easier than just waiting for a call from him.

Sometimes the chief of staff asked me to identify the deceased by their photo from the battlefield. That was easier than coming up with an answer to the midwife's question, 'Will your husband be present during the birth?'

In the end, giving birth yourself is still easier than thinking about when your beloved will be able to see your child for the first time. My life has changed beyond recognition: it's one thing to be a commander, and quite another to have a little commander in you. In December 2022, he was wounded and returned to service on 15 February and on 19 February, I gave birth to our son.

Chapter 13

ONE-WAY TICKET

For security reasons, the interviewee decided not to share his name.

I went into that helicopter with one cigarette and a lighter. From the very beginning, the story looked like I was going to smoke for the last time in my life. Technically, it was easy for the Russians to shoot down our crew. The pilot started to land on the water even before we were shot down, which is what they usually do to mitigate desperation somehow. But the greater the desperation, the more ways the human brain can come up with to be rescued.

Fear is a thing that makes us equal, but what makes us different is plenty of options to act when the first impulse passes.

The guys from our crew fussed and took off their body armour. I was laughing. What are you all hoping for? You can be as inventive as you want, but it's 40 kilometres (25 miles) to the shore, and the water temperature is no higher than 6°C (43°F). Something extraordinary would have to happen for us to survive.

But there is nothing special about the stupidity of the Russian occupiers. Sometimes it allows us to survive. Not far from us, a plane crashed into the water right on the way out.

The crew that took off after ours was shot down with a lot of losses.

One guy was down next to me when he caught a piece of shrapnel. He was bleeding with all the fluids the human body could produce. He tried to say his last words to me and stretched out his arms, but I gently pushed him away from me with an absolute understanding of the situation. I have learned to justify my callousness by the thought that I am acting in the same conditions as unlucky people. Things that help in the here and now contradict public morality and don't make it into a heroic epic.

Anyway, I even should have died earlier near the glass factory in Hostomel. The tank hit my grenade launcher horizontally but missed vertically. It was my second contusion, and I did not understand whether I was lying head up or head down.

Near the Hostomel airfield, our unit had a battle cry. I got tired of carrying the wounded there and simply stopped doing it. This task is impossible to complete. The Russians have armour-piercing bullets, which have extremely high penetration and ricochet. They enter one calf, fly out of it and immediately pierce the other.

There were not many of us there, only my group Ronin's, and Smoke's groups of Special Operations Forces. But we saw what we could do. According to official figures, about fifty Russians were killed in that battle, but there were many more of them. In the end, only Nikita, a Bashkir guy from Ulyanovsk city, survived. He was captured and told us how their documents were taken away and they were taken to Ukraine for 'training'.

I was almost choking on a sandwich when he was given the phone, and his Russian wife asked him 'What are you doing in Ukraine?'

Then we were replaced by border guards with tanks, but they were defeated in four hours, after which Bucha, Irpin, and the Moshchun massacre happened.

My group had every chance of dying in a five-storey building in Irpin, where the Russians were sleeping in the next wing from us, and we didn't even have a grenade launcher. We were so quiet that no one heard us, neither did we hear them. Aerial reconnaissance later showed us pictures. There were five Russian armoured personnel carriers near our campsite.

I was lucky enough to get back with a one-way ticket, and I'm not happy about it.

I am not a patriot. As soon as possible, I will pack my bags and leave this country forever. I don't want to live here anymore, even though I met the enemy with weapons, not at home in shorts. I know all types of un-manned aeriel vehicles (UAV) and ammunition, I am ready to adjust artillery, drones, and aeroplanes, and fire a mortar without calculating, which is why infantry hate people like me. My folks and I come to a position, make noise, and all of us get shot back. There will be shelling anyway, but we at least have reduced the firepower for the Russians to use.

I do not want any military career, no matter what position.

I am not fit for service with my heart disease, kidney disease, and the consequences of injuries. In peacetime, I would not have been allowed to enter the threshold for selection to the special forces.

One day we heard a series of suppressor shots in the neighbouring headblock of Irpin and came across looters. When it was too late to start fighting, the guys from my unit easily jumped over the fence. They are fit and athletic. For two weeks I ate two chocolate bars a day and lost 15 kilograms (33 pounds), but I could not jump over. What a laugh it was when I caught my belt loosely and hung on that fence. Then it fell under me, and we were hit with artillery.

I did not become cruel and did not convince myself that the occupiers were not human. Yes, they are sometimes vile and stupid, but they are still humans. Any devaluation of the enemy leads to defeat. Take Sanya, for example. An ordinary guy from St Petersburg, who even didn't sign a contract. Sanya didn't know that there was a real Third World War scale here. It was he who showed me where and on what broken positions we could harvest Russian electronics. I gave him a cigarette, and he smoked it in just two puffs. So, thanks to Sanya, in the first two weeks of the war, we were able to listen to the negotiations of the enemy through Russian radio stations. In Bucha, we snatched a radio to listen to, having prudently removed human remains from a burning armoured personnel carrier.

A person, who maintains sanity in battle, has a certain level of psychopathy. In war, we involuntarily abandon empathy and put ourselves less and less in another person's shoes. Serving emotions takes a lot of energy, and you need it to survive, at least physically.

I have seen people deny God not because they denied his existence as such, but because the real God could not allow *this*. Or He is a complete psychopath. In the image and likeness of God, we are all psychopaths here... When you don't have special mental disorders, you're less effective during a battle. No wonder people with suicidal tendencies become ideal performers of certain tasks after propaganda treatment while ordinary guys who graduate from ranger schools shit themselves. Regular navy SEALs come off, take pills to concentrate, but run away through the bushes in an unknown direction.

There are two types of soldiers: those who strive to survive, and those who study how to kill more enemies. The paradox is that the latter has a better chance of surviving than those who put the most sense into survival. It's easier to stay alive not when there are few enemies, but when there are not enough enemies for everyone.

A 40-year-old hunter who called himself Kurkul came to us with his 'Saiga' and asked what he had to do. Dmytro, a forester, did not flee to the west in his white Skoda Superb, but drove all our soldiers during the defence of Kyiv in the north-east. If not for him and his car, it is hard to imagine what would have happened there.

Near Irpin, I witnessed two conscripts of the 80th Brigade, each no more than 20 years old, almost fighting. They knew that a Russian armoured personnel carrier was coming, and one of them would have to hit it, and there was only one grenade launcher.

Eighteen-year-old guys who had not had time to taste the life of prosperity, vacation abroad, or family happiness. They are small, round, hung up with equipment, and look like gnomes. And I am in jeans, a jacket, and magazines in my pockets... They looked at our unit, the most elite unit of the Armed Forces of Ukraine, and were surprised. Everything was like in the movies about American special forces, everyone was in civilian clothes, cool and charged. But we simply did not meet the standards that should be in place at least in the special forces.

Every act in war has a name, surname, and pseudonym of a particular person. Not a position, not a rank, not an order. It's pointless to say that the work was done by some brigade. A seemingly unimportant person can leave a company (killed, wounded, transferred), and that company loses its effectiveness once and for all.

It is the deed that bears a person's name, not the other way around. When someone tells you 'I'm a super-secret guy with a super-secret mission and a billion combat exits', you can be sure that this person has not sniffed gunpowder yet. A combat exit can be different. You can go out into the 'dirt', get trapped, sit for three days without ammunition, food, and water, and wait for a small window to escape.

The group of our comrade-in-arms Busya, lieutenant colonel Oleksandr Busko, actively attacked at Soledar. They reached the second line of defence, and they were shot in the back from the first line. Busya is no longer among us after the fighting on the spoil heap. The worst drone video I've seen is of his body on the battlefield.

Mortar battery commander Volodymyr Lobodyuk, call sign Wild, from the 128th Mukachevo Brigade, is a guy with a funny Transcarpathian dialect born in 2000. I came to him to learn how to work with mortars of different calibres, which we found to be useful for the unit. There is nothing to do in this war without something heavy. It seemed quite difficult and risky for us to go to the position and pile on the Russians from the 120th. Wild did it day-in and day-out. For him, it was like brushing his teeth. In addition, mortars are usually fired from the second echelon of defence, and we would drive into a 'grey' zone 0.5 kilometre to the enemy positions, pile up, and quickly escape. We were almost the first such group without a single artilleryman who worked with a mortar.

There are irreplaceable people who go on combat duty, like a shift at McDonald's, and everything is based on them.

Wild was like a fish in water with his mortars, but he had to work without body armour as the PAB2M artillery compass does not like iron. He didn't have any polyethylene or ceramic plates. I did, but only one pair. As a farewell after working together, I gave him my ballistic headphones. Since the ATO, Wild has been commanding a battery of three mortars with his bare ears, even without earplugs.

Wild went to clear the village of Yakovlivka in Donetsk Oblast on 16 December 2022 with everyone else and died ten minutes after being shot. He was the one who should not have gone there because storming is not his profession. Everyone in the war has to do their job, otherwise, there will be trouble. However, that was Wild who dissuaded me from returning for the Mavic. How much does that drone cost? Three thousand dollars? Is your life worth less?

I don't know how much my life is worth, but if I don't go back for that drone, tomorrow someone will go on a sweep without the 'eyes' on top and die. He will take the whole truth with them and leave only guesses behind.

People of war flock to events like moths to light and die very quickly. The world will never know the truth about everything that happened those days. It was privatized by those who did not arrive after our helicopter flight and before us. Those who reached their destination but did not make it home. Those who returned from that flight but found their fate somewhere in Soledar or Barvinkove. Those who came back alive physically, but, like me, dead inside.

P.S. from the author, Oksana Melnyk

One summer morning, my father called me and talked about our distant relative, Oleksandr. His surname is Busko, and there are a lot of people with this name in our big family tree. I probably did not remember him from my childhood, my father assumed. We might have seen each other in early childhood, but my brother must know him.

They used to play football together in the village, when we all were visiting our grandparents in the summer. Both our grandparents' houses are located in the neighborhood. Oleksandr's family moved to different parts of the country and the world. Now, his grandparents' house is empty. Sometimes my granddad Pavlo mows the grass in their yard.

Father said Oleksandr is known as a great guy and a decent military man. He graduated from a military lyceum and an institute and has been defending Ukraine since 2014. He has a wife and kid. He is the real chivalrous type who participated in the famous Azovstal air operation.

It was a series of flights to the besieged city of Mariupol at the beginning of a full-scale invasion in 2022. The operation was to secure an air bridge for the supply of ammunition and medical supplies and to evacuate the wounded. During this operation, the soldiers realized that most likely none of them would return.

Oleksandr fought in various parts of the frontline and died in Soledar in the autumn of 2022. His call sign, Busya, was from his surname.

I suddenly realized that I was familiar with such details, and I knew the story of the one guy with such a call sign. Busya, Soledar, and Mariupol. The story was written at the beginning of 2023.

'Busya is the call sign of Lieutenant Colonel Oleksandr Busko?' I asked my unknown narrator, whom I saw only once and remember just his name.

'Yes, it's him', he answered.

Chapter 14

CATCH UP WITH YOU

The narrator, Serhiy Zhuykov, is managing partner of an investment company in his civilian life. Until 2022, Serhiy managed portfolios for private clients. With the start of the full-scale invasion, he volunteered and took part in the defence of Kyiv, without any combat experience. He co-founded the Sturm Battalion, which later became a separate battalion within the Armed Forces of Ukraine.

My grandfather said almost nothing about the Second World War, but it was there that he began to believe in God. When the village was surrounded, he escaped by climbing into a cesspit up to his neck. That's the first insight when he survived and was not captured.

And once he lit a cigarette in a trench and his comrade asked him for a light. Granddad held out the cigarette butt and an enemy bullet pierced both his cheeks and knocked out two teeth. He had an epiphany. Ultimately.

Some would say it was luck. What a big deal for luck, to be in war...

I try to think less of God. I don't want to disturb Him with trivialities and abuse his attention. It fell near us in the trench again and did not explode. 'German', I said to my fellow comrade, 'it's not just like that. Let's get out of here.'

One day, German and I arrived at a National Guard-related position. We got out of the car and walked away. I suddenly didn't like that the car was facing the blown-up city 12 metres (40 feet) away. I got behind the wheel and drove a bit further.

Then there was a whistle and an explosion. A second one immediately followed. The Russians are very good with mortars. Pieces of concrete and rebar flew in all directions. I heard my comrade's scream. He called for me loudly. The first mine landed where he had stood thirty seconds before and where our car had just been. It was not facing the explosion, but the windscreen had been shattered by the blast. The second one was to the place where my comrade and others had been half a minute before.

In one of the first villages we held, not far from Avdiivka, there was not a single person – only pets scurrying around the road. It was like something out of George Orwell's *Animal Farm*: poultry, bony goats, horses, pigs, purebred dogs, and cats left alone on the farm. It was as if aliens had come, destroyed all the houses and taken all the people to another galaxy.

This was the first village where we saw phosphorus falling from the sky. When it falls on the skin, it causes a very severe burn. A glowing drop of phosphorus burns soft tissue down to the bone. But there was a strong wind blowing and we were not affected by these festive fireworks.

We held this line between two villages for almost a year. Sometimes there was little more than 100 metres (330 feet) between us and the Russians. Constant artillery and mortar shelling, shouting, cursing. The closer you get to the critical moment, the less important it is whether you are a beginner or an expert. You can be a professional, but it won't save you if luck is not on your side today.

Maybe that is why I like my job. In capital management, very little is solved by how well you know the hardware. You must be a professional, but that's not enough for success. Occupiers, looters, and rapists can also be first-rate professionals.

Capital is only the shell of the investment business and just the resource you deal with. But its core is about human values. If you have artificial values, you will be used cynically like a tool. No one will see you as an equal if your values only coincide in market relations.

Sometimes people with a lot of capital have a big heart. For them, money is no longer a test, but a by-product. In the first months of the war, during the defence of Kyiv, I could not communicate regularly with my clients, but almost all of them stayed amidst the chaos. You can blame everything on the situation in the country and global processes, but I am still a manager. I am in one way or another involved in the sinking of their portfolios. However, it was the clients who helped our battalion a lot in the difficult times when Ukraine was given only a few days to resist, and we needed an electronic warfare station and 500,000 hryvnias for it right now.

Now we are being shelled again. Ours have intercepted the Russians' radio transmissions: they are going to hit Clay. It is a position behind a large forest belt near the village of Novobakhmutivka, which is very convenient for sniper support and reconnaissance. But Clay is on a hill, and it is dangerous to work there. To the right, not far away, is Krasnohorivka, which has been fiercely fought over all this time, and the Russians have always tried to break through our defence, attacking non-stop, because this village is of strategic importance on the road to Donetsk.

And now we are all being hit one more time. They will come once, twice, three times... It doesn't matter. The Russians do it every day, several times a day. They have no shortage of ammunition.

The mines are laid a metre apart, like a chessboard. There is nothing to breathe, just clouds of smoke with gunpowder and dust.

When the blast stops, I must get up, shake off the dry earth and run across the railway tracks, constantly in the sights of enemy snipers. This short distance takes forever. Beyond the tracks is a viaduct, and beyond the viaduct is the small forest. In this tunnel, our group stops to catch their breath. Our group always stops in this tunnel, and the whole platoon lives here, holding two important positions.

It is scorching hot. We are sweating, dirty, and tired. Some of us haven't had rotation for a year. Millionaires and ordinary people, university graduates and street people, businessmen and unemployed, believers and atheists, military and civilians, scum and saints.

And me. I ran and survived. I can breathe. Happiness has become closer and easier. You don't have to chase it. If you run across the tracks, it will catch up with you itself.

Everyone is joyful that nothing happened, and we are all safe and sound. We laugh at silly jokes. Someone has made tea; someone is drinking water or energy drink. Someone has headphones on and is listening to music. Someone is looking at their children – at least in a photo. Someone is planning for tomorrow and how to make sure that we are not the ones who are going to be hurt.

A little while later, the adrenaline rush subsides. The silence around becomes oppressive and hard to trust in. Doubt and anger set in. One of the guys asks why we are sitting here. No one supports us, no one replaces us. What's the point of all this...?

But no one gets up and leaves. Long conversations are inappropriate here. No one is interested in success or personal growth. There is no place for great gurus or professional motivators.

War does not change us fundamentally. It just exposes the soul in the same way that power and money do. Scoundrels remained scoundrels. Good people remain good. War only brings out all the things we have not used under the illusion of a safe life or ignorance.

Ordinary men could do what titans could not. They have different motivations for fighting: some have nowhere to go, some have lost jobs and families. But they are here, and their risks are not phantom. They were able to do it and the former masters of life were not. On 24 February 2022, spiritual mentors, gurus, and success promoters disappeared from the airwaves, along with their advice on how to achieve happiness, success, how to become a real man or woman, how to live consciously, etc. I did not meet any of them in the war.

A happy person does not think about what happiness is every day. A successful person does not invent recipes for success. If you are financially secure, you don't think about money all the time.

When you feel love, you don't have to think about what it is. If you have God in your life, you don't have to look for him.

Once I was driving past a small town on the frontline. I was driving fast, but I managed to see a teenage girl on the side of the road. She stood with her hands over her face.

It was late November. It was cold and wet outside. There was a muddy mess and rainwater under the wheels. I drove about a kilometre down the road and turned towards the girl by the side of the road. She was clutching her knees and crying. Her pet cat was lying motionless next to her.

She said that the cat had been hit by a car.

'Let's bury him here by the road', I said. She agreed. I got a shovel, and we talked as I dug the hole. The girl was 13, one year younger than my daughter. She had brightly coloured hair and brightly lacquered nails for the first time. She lives with her mother, who lost her job after the full-scale invasion started. Her father is absent, and it is not clear if he was ever there. She dreams of going to the shopping centre, but it is closed because the town is suffering from Russian bombing. We talked about everything and then her mother came and thanked me through tears.

About three weeks passed. I was driving along the same road and saw that girl with a small puppy. It's so strange... It's at moments like this that you realize that life goes on even amid this horror.

We have no idea how little we need. We think that these things should be a priori, but they are very fragile. When you can go to the cinema or city park. When you see your children. When there is laughter. When you can go on a trip. When all your relatives are alive and well, and your 'own' are close by. When people are doing great things in your country, not somewhere across the ocean. When you can be alone at the seaside or walk in the mountains.

When you follow your own path, no matter how difficult it is, you are happy. Despite the horrors around you, you become happier in the war, perhaps than you have been in your whole life.

Chapter 15

RUBICON

Ihor Zhaloba is a doctor of historical sciences, senior research fellow at the Institute of History of Ukraine of the National Academy of Sciences of Ukraine, professor of the Department of International Relations at Borys Grinchenko Kyiv University, and president of the Pan-European Union of Ukraine. With the beginning of the full-scale invasion, Ihor Zhaloba joined the Territorial Defence of Kyiv. The professor lectures not only to students but also to his colleagues in the service in the aerial reconnaissance team.

My friends from the scientific community abroad have emailed me to say that they are deeply concerned, shocked, and do not know what to do. When people say something like that, they have several options, but one of them requires permission: from within, to control the situation; from without, if they need to share responsibility.

My daughters and I had taken a course for civilians to be prepared for possible combat. (In Europe, I have friends who condemned me for that: why so radical? There are those who, since the start of the full-scale invasion, have apologized for their past fascination with Putin. These are mostly the same people.)

I had a full tank and a can of diesel fuel and was supposed to evacuate my daughters immediately, but things turned out differently than I planned. The city was jammed with traffic.

'Girls, I don't know what will happen to us. I don't know where we're going to go and when we're going to get there.'

'Dad, let's go home. If we turn there, we won't get out of the traffic jam. Everything is blocked.'

'You sure?'

'Yeah. Let's go home.'

It is hard to convey our happiness after we returned home together. My English is frankly worse than my German, so I asked my younger daughter Sophia to help with the response to that concerning mail.

'So, write it down like this. First, we are not shocked here. Second, we know what to do.'

My last lecture before the full-scale invasion was devoted to the civilizational choice of Ukrainians. My students and I talked about how our fate would become clear the next day. But when the time came, everything changed by the minute.

Two days later I received the machine gun and felt more joyful than the day I got married. I did not plan to ask God for an indulgence to shoot a Russian soldier who came here to kill. Does it make any difference why he came here with a gun? To kill, to steal someone's toilet and washing machine, or even if he had a plan to burn down St Sophia's Cathedral in Kyiv. He crossed our border illegally in a tank. This person should not be here. After all, I have children. So does God. He must understand. I'm sure that if Jesus Christ had walked the streets of the occupied towns of Bucha and Irpin, no Russian soldier would have bothered with a crucifix. He would have been shot in the middle of a street like the Ukrainian civilians who couldn't get evacuated.

Almost everyone in our territorial defence unit in Kyiv was a civilian, except for the commander. Some were interested in the military, some were not. Some had never held a gun before, others had never fired one. Master Sergeant Oleksiy was very angry because we were slow to learn: one of his legs was in a cast, and he had to jump up and down on crutches several times to teach us something.

We are embarrassed for our fallen soldiers. We were often saved by some providence and enthusiasm. When there was heavy shelling and heavy losses in neighbouring units, we had no wounded.

One day I had to go on night duty with my comrades Sam and Beast at 2.00 am. Sam was late, which was annoying for me, a lecturer in civilian life. While I was waiting for Sam, the Russians started bombing us with 'grads'. We all fell to the ground together, and the grads fell exactly where we would have stood if Sam hadn't been late. The enemy's fire hit an oak tree right next to where our guys were standing. The vehicles were so badly damaged that they turned into sieves. But the fuel and ammunition did not explode. Surprisingly, the next day our leaky vehicles worked as if nothing had happened.

Tanker Mykyta Zoryanyi was sleeping soundly in a metal trailer with other soldiers, tired of the anxious days of war. Suddenly the trailer was hit by a Russian missile. The guys were miraculously not burned alive. None of them was even wounded. I came across Mykyta Zoryanyi accidentally a year after that at a petrol station along the road, while I was on my way to write reports.

'Mykyta? Zoryanyi?'

'Ihor?'

'How are you?'

'I'm fine, I just don't know how many cat lives I have left.'

'My friend, I was worried about you.'

'Unfortunately, not without reason. A lot has happened since then. My tank burned down.'

'What about Volodya? Is he okay?'

'Volodya is no longer with us...'

Sometimes I think about things, trying to find the answer to how the boys survived the missile, and why Mykyta happened to be on this road and at this particular petrol station. Mykyta could have stopped anywhere, but for some reason, he ended up here at this very moment: ten seconds in time and 10 metres (30 feet) in space and we would have missed each other, perhaps forever.

Mykyta and I hugged each other, hoping that we would meet again. Nothing bad happened to us and we met by chance due to some unknown circumstances that I cannot explain – neither as a historian, nor as a military man, nor as a human being.

I only have a vision that we as a society started thinking in the same direction, using the same words, and cursing our killers with the same phrases. We began to act in sync and walk the same paths, as if we had one body for all of us.

We became angry beyond words. It was much more than anger. It was something stronger, and it spread evenly throughout the body of our people. A regular human being cannot be so angry and so eager to throw off the shackles and tear his executioner to pieces. Even if that executioner is Goliath and you have only a stone in your hand.

Some say Russian soldiers are poorly trained and that their advantage is only in numbers. On the news, people saw the toothless faces of Russian soldiers who were captured by our army. Is this the 'world's second army'? Are they homeless, convicts, or alcoholics? Do they really know how to hold a gun?

Yes, they do, and there are a lot of them. My commander, Ihor Koval, was killed near Bakhmut by an armed occupier, and it doesn't matter who was the murderer, what his level of intelligence was, whether he was drunk or sober, or whether he was serving a sentence for a crime before he was mobilized. And on the same day as Ihor's funeral, the life of Kyiv historian and tour guide Serhiy Myronov was cut short. Serhiy became famous for restoring old doors in the historic districts of our city on his own. He was seriously wounded in the war and did not survive. Such people are always the first to go into battle. They, along with thousands of incredibly talented and decent people, were killed by armed and trained Russian soldiers.

While we were waiting for help with weapons, a lot of people died; not just people, but specialists who will be missed in the future. I enjoy teaching a course on the history of international relations, and I understand how all this happened and why we waited so long for weapons. This understanding does not ease my pain for all those we have lost.

But now we are creating the kind of army my late commander dreamed of. I dreamed of such an army too, and now I see the changes that other nations have been making for decades. We have a conceptual understanding of our experience, and I see this not only as a soldier but also as a scientist.

When I was writing my dissertation and working with the research of Western experts, I realized how important this is. In Soviet times, we were taught a universal cliché that relieved us of responsibility for conceptual understanding: 'The work is based on Marxist-Leninist ideology'. Nobody understood what that meant. And it didn't matter that there were no thinkers in the Soviet Union who understood Marxism – the real one, not its vulgarized substitute. There were no thinkers who understood what it meant: ideas that take hold of the masses become the locomotives of history.

The path of our people has been so thorny that there is no room for clichés in our conceptual understanding.

Too many people have crossed the Rubicon.

Too many people left here forever.

Too many people left a comfortable life abroad and went to war. Too many people remained on the battlefield forever or until the Ukrainians recaptured the land and exhumed it.

Too many people realized that they had not lived before 24 February.

Too many people can talk all evening about how they accidentally survived.

Too many people woke up from the explosions not with fear of the enemy, but of the unknown.

I expected our president to say this in one of his keynote speeches on the anniversary of the full-scale invasion. He said that the Russian invasion came as a surprise to the entire Ukrainian people. The president did not say a word about the fact that while Ukraine was being stormed by the Russians, while the frightened former lords of life and corrupt officials were storming the western borders in the hope of staying in Europe, people with no combat experience were storming the military recruitment offices. There was not just a lot of them, but a critical mass.

I was waiting for the president to speak about this, but he did not.

Michael Gahler, a member of the European Parliament, and I had a conversation about this at a conference in Nuremberg.

'Ihor, I'm going to be in Kyiv tomorrow and I'm meeting with a lot of people. What would you like to convey to the president? Now you have this opportunity to say a word to him through me.'

'Tell him that we all don't need someone from above to reassure us. I want a frank conversation. We in Ukraine can make decisions at the speed of light. We are already forging a new quality of state governing based on the scientific and technological revolution, and this is not yet the case in many very developed countries. But as soon as we have a frank conversation, we will turn everything upside down.'

At my last lecture in peaceful Kyiv, we also talked about how long the war would last. There has never been a single empire in history that did not suffer a painful collapse, but even if Russia collapses one day, our common borders with its people will not disappear. We have to rebuild our entire lives, our world views, our relationships, and, above all, ourselves. Everyone will have to choose: to leave, to stay, to join the fight, to supply ammunition, to stand on the sidelines and wait for it to be over, to complain about how bad things are.

We Ukrainians tend to complain about how bad everything is around us, how bad our roads are, and how low the quality of life is in our country. However, this opinion is similar to nostalgia for Soviet ice cream and cheap sausage: it's long gone, and everyone has forgotten what it tastes like, but people like to talk about it.

Ukrainians have done as much at home in three decades as it took other nations in 300 years. Not because we are special, but because we don't have that much time. There is no such fierce resistance out of the blue – this is not an eyewitness and participant in the events, but a historian speaking outside of me. If this had not happened, all the predictions about Russian tanks in the centre of Kyiv would have come true in three days, as predicted in the West.

I remember missionaries at various conferences telling us about European values and how we would never be successful unless we embodied them. But suddenly they shit their pants and turned out to be incapable of following the lifestyle they were promoting. They shit themselves about Putin: 'Not everything is so clear', 'the issue needs discussion', and so on. They shit because of the Ukrainians who started to fight for the values that Europe has monopolized. And not only to fight for rights but also to fulfil responsibilities, even if it costs lives.

In the last historical process, previous generations had time and leeway for 'buffer' processes and grey tones. Today all processes are accelerated. Everyone's world in this country has become black and white.

My German friend Benedikt once said that we Ukrainians have always been prone to extremes.

'You never recognized half-tones. Only *"Nein oder Ja* [yes or no]"', he said.

The truth is that wars are never won in shades of grey. Grey tones do not encourage you to leave your comfort zone and take action. They don't help you give up your current way of life or change anything. Grey tones tolerate indifference. They make you think about how to deal with Putin, to rate him on a ten-point scale, to make you cling to the price of fuel and to a modest, well-fed, and protected life. It's easy to get lost in grey tones.

Chapter 16

SIN

Serhiy Dmitriyev, call sign Padre, is an officer of the military chaplaincy service of the Territorial Defence Forces of the Armed Forces of Ukraine, and a priest of the Orthodox Church of Ukraine. He initiated the opening of the Wall of Remembrance near St Michael's Golden-Domed Cathedral and founded the Eleos-Ukraine Charity Foundation which helps the victims of hostilities. An interesting thing about Padre is that he was born in Russia.

'Is killing a sin?'

Murder is when you hack the old woman, Alyona Ivanovna, who rents you a room, with an axe. And also her sister-in-law, Elizaveta. And then you frantically wipe the blood stains on your coat.

It is a virtue to defend your family and loved ones with arms.

I saw four-dozen Ukrainian women who had been raped by Russians being brought to the city hospital. One girl was only 18 years old and had been raped continuously for eight days in a row. I don't want to comment on the commandment 'thou shalt not kill' anymore. I have a daughter; she is 21. As a husband and as a father, I will not hesitate for a moment – I will shoot the Russian rapist.

'Is it a sin to recant?'

When the Russians came to Crimea in 2014, I was a priest of the Moscow Patriarchate. I came out to the parishioners after the Sunday sermon and made an announcement. 'I can't do this anymore. I am leaving the church of the Moscow Patriarchate. I will move to the Ukrainian church. Those who disagree with me can leave the church.'

Almost no one left the church. People even admitted that they were waiting for this moment. Just one family left the church and stopped attending services.

A temple is not yet a church, but only a building in which people gather to witness their presence to God. The church is people.

'Is it a sin to condemn?'

It is not enough to condemn. The Vatican holds a microphone with one hand and preaches sermons about peace, and with the other hand, it presents the Peace Prize to Putin. Yes, he received it in 2015, after the annexation of Crimea.

Condemning is not just a little. It is nothing. When Russians burned down someone's house in Irpin, they burned down your house in Brussels. When they raped a woman in Bucha, they raped you somewhere in London. If you killed someone's husband at the front, they killed yours in New York. They robbed someone's house in Borodyanka – they took everything from your apartment in Tokyo.

What will you do after all this? Will you just condemn the robber? Will you express your concern that you were raped? Will you be deeply concerned that your house was burned down?

'Is it a sin not to forgive?'

Let a woman who was raped by the Russian occupier answer. Let the crippled children speak. Let our soldiers who are now in Russian captivity speak. Let our soldiers who have been released from Russian captivity speak. Let the boys and girls in hospitals speak up. Widows and orphaned children. Parents whose sons and daughters were taken away from them. Let the mother answer who comes to St Michael's Golden-Domed Monastery and spends hours near the Wall of Memory watching her dead son's photo on it. I do not know who this mother is, although I may have known her son. But she is the one who has the right to answer.

'Is it a sin not to tithe to the church?'

SIN

When my community and I were still subordinate to the Moscow Patriarchate, I worked for social service. It was very difficult to help. It was difficult to get permission from the top, difficult to communicate with bureaucrats and corrupt officials in cassocks. I heard a lot from the bishops. Some give you money to help – you give me part of it in cash. I mentally told them to go to Hell.

'Is abortion a sin?'

A Ukrainian girl got pregnant by a Russian soldier. She was raped by the occupier. The girl's mother is a very religious person. She doesn't want her child to have an abortion and suggests leaving the child in an orphanage. The father of the pregnant girl is against it. The priest of the Moscow Patriarchate advised her to give birth.

The pregnant girl is only 12 years old. She is in the sixth grade of a secondary school. Will this priest have the strength of mind to help children – a schoolgirl and her newborn baby – for the rest of their lives, as long as they need it? To buy nappies and baby formula? Or will he only have enough for advice?

Often people come to a pastor for advice when they have already made a decision. They don't need indictments; they don't need prohibitions. People need to know that they are not left alone with their decisions.

I suggest you don't do this, and I will stand by you in your choice.

I suggest you do it, and I will stand by you in your choice.

Actions, not advice – this is the way of the pastor.

'Is atheism a sin?'

God does not need mediators. He does not need a church. He does not need a church for faith. He does not need our ritualism either. He does not need us in church on Sunday. The only ones who need it are us.

In this restaurant, I am just a waiter who serves food and does not always get a tip. But I am not a psychologist. A psychologist helps a person to take off their cross and thus makes life easier. The church is a force that helps you to have reliable support.

Those who were atheists before the war received proof of their belief, because all this cannot happen in a world where there is a God. But those who believed also received clear evidence of their conviction that there is a God. Because all this cannot happen in a world where there is no God.

My girlfriend is an atheist. This does not prevent us from loving each other.

'Is suicide a sin?'

I know soldiers who have committed suicide. I feel guilty that I was not there and could not do anything.

'Is it a sin not to pray?'

At a time when prayer is becoming a weapon, you have to pray with a machine gun in your hands.

'Is foul language a sin?'

They say, 'We are Russians, God is with us.' God is not with you. You have a dick with you.

'Is war a sin?'

War always ends in love. If love has not yet come, then the war is not over.

Chapter 17

PIGEON MAIL

The story of Kyrylo Babentsov, call sign Cobra, was recorded in January 2015, when Kyrylo was defending the village of Pisky in Donetsk Oblast within a volunteer battalion of the Organization of Ukrainian Nationalists (OUN). He has been at war since the beginning of the anti-terrorist operation in Donbas. His story reveals the details of the first year of the war in Donbas.

On the eve of the full-scale invasion, Kyrylo was working abroad, but he returned and defended the state as a commander of a combat group of the Carpathian Sich volunteer unit. He died of a wound sustained in the battle for the city of Irpin in Kyiv region in March 2022. He was 31 years old at the time of his death.

In fact, we do not exist. We are not registered, and our fighters receive neither salaries nor any social guarantees, nor the status of combatants. Even when fighters of the OUN battalion are admitted to hospital after being shot or wounded by shrapnel, they were registered with the words 'domestic trauma', 'accident', or something similar.

People often join the military for the sake of looting, arrogance, and career. The army is often stuffed with people who have no desire to defend the state. We have only a fighting spirit, strict discipline, and a fight against bad habits, and there is nothing that could attract such people. We even lack drinking water and fuel, not to mention military equipment and weapons. But we have not yet died of hunger, because volunteers are constantly bringing us something. Everything our battalion has is given to us by ordinary people. Everything we have, use in battle, eat – it is the work of volunteers. We receive nothing from the state. But even if we did... Sometimes the weapons that the guys from the Armed Forces of Ukraine have are unusable.

While I was living a peaceful life in Kyiv, I hardly ever dreamed, and now I dream almost every night. I dreamt about the Donetsk airport (DAP) even when I hadn't been there yet. I was obsessed with Donetsk airport. It attracted volunteers like a magnet. Only the hottest minds and those who proved themselves best were sent there. These are real battles at the call of the heart. At Donetsk airport, the opportunity to fight for Ukraine was greater than anywhere else.

The landscapes of the Sands remind me of screenshots from the game STALKER.[10] This is what the 'Russian world' leads to. People here are left to their own devices. There is no administration, no medical care, no shops in Pisky. There is no gas, no electricity, no pensions... Those who are still here live off the help of the Ukrainian military – from us and other units. They also receive food, clothes, and sometimes our electricity.

Most people are silent about their position on the future of our country. In contrast to those who openly thank us for our protection and assistance, people who remain silent make it clear to us that they hate us. Of course, they are ready to collaborate. While the village of Pisky was occupied by Russian forces, no one fled. They lived their lives and were happy with everything. But when the hostilities started, when the struggle for territories began, they began to whine, saying that they were being 'killed', 'bombed', etc. And they were not concerned about any fundamental aspects. Now they are only concerned that a bomb might fall on their heads, or their house might burn down, and they don't care whose government is in charge. The main thing is that it all ends as soon as possible, and they do not care who will be the winner.

I quickly adapted to this way of life and the fact of permanent death around me. Contact battles are rare. Sometimes there are 'skirmishes' with sabotage groups, but this war as such is a continuous bombardment. Tanks, artillery, hail, mortars... I am not afraid of shelling – I am only terrified of the cruelty.

There was a case when a grenade killed a guy, and his body was badly mutilated. The military medics did not want to take him. We collected him together with the medics of the Dnipro-1 Battalion. Recently, an armored personnel carrier of the armed forces was blown up. The driver was blown up, and the rest of the crew miraculously survived. The body of the deceased was supposedly taken away. But when I had to climb into that armored personnel carrier a few days later to see if there was anything of value left, I saw the remains of his organs, even one severed leg. I took it all out, put it in a bag, and brought it to the headquarters.

'I brought your soldier. What should we do with this? We have to bury him somehow. We can't just leave it to rot.'

'But we don't know what to do since it is the winter.'

'Then let me leave it to you, we need to figure it out. It's not right for dogs to eat the body of a warrior.'

'Oh no, you don't need to leave anything here. We'll make a call now.'

Then they called somebody in charge, who ordered them to give the bag to the medics of a volunteer unit.

When I talk to those who live in the peaceful capital, they are more concerned about us than we are about ourselves. But we are really living a normal life. Many young guys like it. Here we could do something important, to fight evil, and not just earn and spend money in a vicious circle, as it is in civilian life.

I'm here to prevent the scum from taking our Donbas and, after Donbas, Kharkiv or Dnipro. I want my native Odesa to remain part of Ukraine forever. Because if they take one thing, they will go further. To change anything, we need to get rid of the old vestiges of Soviet agents and put war criminals in jail under the laws of wartime. We have to stop it all, and we will when everyone is in their place.

Sometimes, when I do get a connection, I call my mother and ask her to tell all my family and friends that I am fine. There is almost no connection – you can't call everyone. Recently, my friends went home for rotation, and I stayed here in Pisky. Through my friends, I sent a letter to my girlfriend that I had written by hand. My friend could only send it to me when he was at home in Lviv. There is no internet, and this pigeon mail is the only way to say more than 'alive and well'.

Chapter 18

KISSED BY GOD

Natalia Borysovska is a senior sergeant and squadron leader of the reconnaissance platoon. After defending the country in the anti-terrorist operation, she tried but couldn't return to civilian life. Natalia dreams of a house, three children, and her animal shelter.

One winter evening my parents and I were warming ourselves by the stove in Granny's house in Khmelnytskyi. A film about the second Russian-Chechen war was on TV.

'Dad, is war possible here?'

'Of course, it is. Not only possible, but it definitely will happen.'

'So, one day we will start the same as they did?'

'Wars do not start in one day. We have been defending ourselves for centuries. It is inevitable.'

I joined the army when I was 20 years old.

War is not a female issue, although women's things help to rescue in war. I have a bunch of dresses and heels that travelled in my old army backpack throughout Donbas years ago when this war was called the anti-terrorist operation. I used to go on dates in civilian clothes between combat exits and relax that way.

But war is not a male thing either. Hands that have learned to hold a penis are not necessarily capable of holding a weapon. When they were pointing a machine gun at me with trembling hands, I saw in front of me just a man trying to show himself as a man. He didn't seem like a warrior.

Sometimes women came to our battalion, and I interviewed each of them. These were typical conversations.

'Why do you want to do this?'

'I want to defend Ukraine and its nation.'

'You lie.'

'Seriously, I'm a patriot.'

'Just admit you need a husband. Let me marry you off, and that's it… No need to join if you're a woman who just cannot meet the right person or find an aim to live a civilian life.'

The chief of staff was outraged at me after those conversations.

'You're weeding everyone out. We can't boast of having women in our brigade because of you!'

He was right. Shortly afterward, when I joined another brigade, they recruited two dozen women. But that man was not happy for long.

'One of the girls is pregnant, the other one drinks, and another one can't stay off a penis. There is also a drug addict.'

War has no genitals. It is impossible to be a woman here and you can't be a man either.

When the war broke out, I had to look for a long time to get to Donbas. Our unit was not sent to the east at all. When I asked to go to war, the commander said 'Girl, calm down.'

Once I had the offer to become a sniper. That sounded aesthetically pleasing, a girl sniper. But by that time, I knew myself enough to refuse. I am too emotional for this position.

Military service is not about heroism, it's about a profession. When a person is operated on, the doctor seems to be a hero. Somebody's whole life depends on him. When a house is on fire, a firefighter becomes a hero – you can't do without him. I don't like it when people call us heroes, as I do what I get paid for. This is my duty, not heroism. Heroism begins where professionalism ends, which is acquired through military training.

I first came to Donbas as a clerk. It was 2014 and it was my first time seeing bombed-out towns and villages. There, I saw the concept of a woman in the army differently.

Our bus stopped on the way to the east for a break to go to the toilet, breathe, and smoke. I went towards the boarding area. I looked back and saw a few guys following me.

'We will guard you.'

'You guys? From what?'

'What if there's a tripwire?'

'So, if you see that, you have only machine guns, boys.'

But it was about something else. They had mothers, sisters, wives, girlfriends, female friends... women for whom they are here. They cannot help but care about women. This is not a machine gun that can be fired or not. This thing is built into them. If they did not have this thing built in, they would not be able to fight. This makes men unconsciously care for women all their lives, and save them, even if they may die because of that.

In early 2015, during a mission in Vuhlehirsk, I spent a day lying on something cold. At that time, I had already stopped working in clerical work and was engaged in reconnaissance. I started bleeding internally connected with the reproductive system. My comrades dragged me to the district hospital in Svitlodarsk. It was a typical gynaecological department of the district centre. There was a bunch of women in that hospital whose husbands were fighting on the other side of the barricades. I was put in a separate ward.

The woman who was deputy chief doctor and her daughter took turns visiting me. That woman confessed to me that she was not so much against the Russians as against Ukraine. But her 9-year-old daughter sings Ukrainian songs for me. I'm lying with a drip, hugging my Mickey Mouse, a stuffed toy my grandmother gave me when I was 5. My grandmother whose house we spent cold winter evenings in died just before the war. I still wake up at night when I feel my toy is not there.

For some reason, my boys came back. The doctor wouldn't let them see me.

'Give our girl back.'

'I can't, the bleeding doesn't stop.'

'Move away or I'll shoot you!'

I was taken to Vuhlehirsk. The Debaltseve cauldron was starting. There was massive shelling. I was sitting in the basement. Then the news showed a hospital in Svitlodarsk, where I was lying for several days. A shell hit the wing and the ward where I was supposed to be.

People often say I am being kissed by God. Death has passed me and people around me so many times that I couldn't help believing it. I like to joke about death. The jokes about death must be confident and loud so that it hears everything, calls you insane, and avoids you.

My friend got hit by a mine. It was a terrible accident.

'Your balls still there?'

'Yeah.'

'You remember, I'm supposed to be the godmother of your kids.'

My parents have always reproached me for my tattoos. I have fourteen of them, some of them done by myself. Mum and Dad still believe that I can remove them with vinegar.

'Why did you do all this?'

'Mum, what if it's not my leg they put into the coffin? And with tattoos, it's very convenient to put everything together!'

My husband likes to joke about it too.

'Someday after your death, your fancy tattooed skin will be used to make gorgeous wallets and purses. They will cost millions!'

'Someday? I need millions now!'

'...'

'When are you going to propose to me? We are both military "men"! Suddenly something happens, 15 million is not lying on the road...'

When we were laughing at death, it was always somewhere nearby.

I think the old mole Death whispered something like, 'What idiots', didn't want to have anything in common with us, and walked away.

Some people have a well-worn road to life with age, while others have a road to death, which every time they come up, scratch their temple with their index finger, and move on.

They say that when a mine falls near you and doesn't explode you can be born again. Or wake up if you live as if in a dream. I thought a lot about what I had missed during these nine years of my life. What I didn't do for myself, but did for people. Those people could afford to sleep until the morning of 24 February 2022 because I hadn't slept for nine years before that.

In February 2022, our unit was transferred from Donbas to Kyiv to work in the Bucha, Irpin, and Moshchun areas. I felt uneasy when I first heard sirens and explosions in Kyiv.

When we were there, I thought a lot about why I chose this path. I missed the moment when I could have enjoyed motherhood. In February 2022, my husband and I were planning to go to Kyiv to do IVF. I still don't know what kind of mother I'm supposed to be. I started fighting for my health. I am exhausted, both physically and psychologically. I gave my Mickey Mouse to my parents in case something happened to me.

But I would never have become me if it weren't for all this. I would never have met the people who are with me now. My husband is also a military man. Anton had been watching me for a long time, but he could not decide to meet me. There must always be a dragon on the way to a woman. If a woman is a soldier, the dragon is her commander. My commander is like a father to me. And a father commander is an even bigger obstacle for suitors than just a dragon or a father.

But once upon a time, the commander asked Anton to take me to Dnipro. I was dating one guy at that time whom I knew a long time and decided to try a relationship. Anton took me to Dnipro to that man and went home to Melitopol.

I had a wonderful evening in Dnipro with wine and a delicious dinner. But when we started talking about politics with that guy, I immediately packed my things and flew out of the house. I found a taxi.

'Take me to Melitopol.'

'But it's 340 kilometres away…'

'It doesn't matter. Just take me.'

That's not my style. There were a lot of friends in Dnipro with whom I could stay for the night. Anton also had a date that night.

When I arrived, he took me to his grandmother's house. That's where I fell asleep.

I woke up feeling very warm, with someone covering me and stroking my head.

'Listen, I'm going to the city for a while. I must go on business.'

'Yes, of course, I'll be here.'

He left. I opened my eyes. I still felt a little sick from last night's wine and the night's drive. I was the only one in the house, except for my grandmother. It was hard to explain to myself why I was here. I had nothing better to do than shake out the carpets and clean the whole house.

When Anton arrived, I made dinner. We talked until late into the night. The next day he asked me to start going out with him. My life began from a new page.

A lot of things have come out now. It's calmer now, and I can let myself cry as much as I want. It used to be so hard that I used to take a pillow, bury my face in it, and scream with all my might. I have been in the army for thirteen years. No one has ever seen me cry before. I started embroidering, drawing, and saying no. I don't want to be remembered as a woman who gave her life to the war. I want to do something else – something creative.

I used to think that people say I am 'kissed by God' because I and everyone around me is spared death. But not only that. Sometimes I ask myself what this whole journey is worth. If not for him, I would never have known love. Or I would have, but it would have been completely different. Maybe I would have been carried in his arms, but that's for cheap melodramas. Being carried around in someone's arms is nothing compared to being thrown up to the sky with those arms.

Chapter 19

DONTWHINE

Leonid Ostaltsev, the call sign Dandelion, is a Ukrainian military officer and entrepreneur, junior sergeant of the Armed Forces of Ukraine, and a participant in the Russian-Ukrainian war. He is the founder of the Pizza Veterano group, the business project to help military personnel returning from war adapt to civilian life.

I was standing in Mariinsky Park, dressed in a costume in the shape of a slice of pizza. Adults laughed, and their children threw small stones at me. The worst thing was that it was 2008, I was just 21, and girls were making fun of me.

That day, my friend asked me to cover for him at work for a day or two. He was handing out leaflets for some pizzerias near the Arsenalna metro station. I had on that suit all day and promised myself that I would never again deal with pizza in my life.

When I took the suit back to the pizzeria, an Azerbaijani man was sitting there, and a very beautiful waitress was on his lap. We managed to get a few words about nothing. The guy looked so arrogant, as if he had grabbed God by the beard, ripped it out, and put it on his chin.

'Let me teach you how to make pizza.'

'Who are you anyway?'

'Do you care? I'm a pizza chef. Let me show you something.'

Rafael Agayev, aka Raf, was the person who made me discover dough.

I got a job in this pizza restaurant and worked in the kitchen for several years. Raf was one of the people who helped me find my dream job in a place where it was impossible to do. Some people work with only one thought in mind to get the day over with. I spent twelve to fourteen hours per day, and six days a week in the kitchen. It's always noisy and every minute there is a risk of suffocation from the heat of the ovens. But I would leave thinking about how I would come back here tomorrow and do what I love again.

Raf and I both went to war in 2014. We came back in the summer of 2015 and checked together whether we still knew how to make pizza. We were very surprised when it turned out that the dough still remembers us.

Then I wrote my first business plan on my knees, having just $50 in my pocket. My wife was eight months pregnant, and I didn't know how to go on.

I started to look for money with all my might, pestered everyone, and got twenty-two refusals. But the twenty-third person suddenly astounded me. There was an unprofitable restaurant in the Metrograd Shopping Centre on Maidan Nezalezhnosti in the underground passage. Why not try? He invested about $4,000 and bought ovens and tables. He even made it rent-free. This is how the first Veterano pizzeria appeared in 2015. People liked it from the beginning. The guys who came back from Donbas did not give up, did not fall into depression, opened a place, and baked pizza themselves.

Our Margarita was so shitty at first that I'm still ashamed of it. However, people came and queued up for it. We ran out of dough, which we had prepared in advance, at 4.00 pm. I told people that there was no more dough, it had to rise for twelve hours, so come back tomorrow. People were not interested in cooking techniques and just wanted their pizza. They liked what was happening then. It's much easier to support two guys with happy faces covered with flour than drunk, depressed men with no hope for the future and a lot of accusations against civilians.

No one likes to feel guilty, and our pizzeria was a place where civilians did not feel indebted to the military. At the same time, it was a place where the military people found themselves in civilian life after returning home.

Two months later, the pizzeria reached the break-even point, and in 2017, it moved to separate premises on Sofiivska Street. Veterano is a franchise that any war veteran can get, and anyone can work here, both civilians and military.

War is a litmus test. It has all the conditions to realize how alive you are because it is there that you see how mortal you are. Before I heard the sounds of the explosions, I didn't want kids and never imagined myself as a father. But today I have a son. It is a small copy of me, and I already know that he will have a very difficult life.

People return to civilian life differently. They no longer want to do what they used to do in their lives. They are looking for new meanings, new work, and new vocations. And you have two extremes: to withdraw into yourself and degrade or to deny this fact and do something with your life. This is possible only if you are not afraid of failure. When you come back from the frontline, your fear moves you instead of stopping you. The worst thing that can happen is that you will fail, but finally, you still will be safe and sound.

You won't make a Margarita, but you won't lose an arm or a leg. The dough will not rise, but you will still come home. You have been refused money for your business for the hundredth time, but no one forbids you to apply for the 101st time. There's always a chance to live happily ever after, even if you've taken a risk and failed.

In ordinary life, you don't get run over by an infantry fighting vehicle on the road, as it was in Pisky in 2015. The artillery didn't kill me, the separatists didn't kill me, and for some reason, one guy decided to go somewhere urgently during the shelling by the IFV I was hiding under during the shelling. My life did not flash before my eyes. I just thought it could be the most stupid death in the war. Vasya, my comrade-in-arms, had his heel blown off.

Uncle Yura caught 150 pieces of shrapnel. He always said, 'Don't whine, you f**cking bastard!' That's why we called him 'Dontwhine'. Now, Uncle Yura is doing well. Sometimes the boys and I visit him for tea.

Most of us who returned from the ATO in Donbas understood that Russia would attack on a large scale. This understanding does not require exceptional mental abilities, it is just about causes and effects.

As long as you are healthy, you do not value your health. No one needs independence until someone tries to take it away. Until 2014, we did not know what to do with it. Even on 24 February 2022, not everyone realized what was happening around them. I was driving past the city and saw people walking slowly between the stalls at the market and buying something. A few days later, the city, littered with abandoned cars, almost died out. As a pizzeria owner, I received calls from some people asking where they could get 500,000 tonnes of flour because the factory was out of commission and in a few days, there would be no bread left in Kyiv.

The pizzeria that Raf and I started with him has always gathered veterans within its walls. And then it turned into a headquarters for the military where brothers-in-arms met and found each other, and where they agreed on common affairs, got to know each other, planned, and helped.

Raf gave his life in the battle for Ukraine near Mariupol on 8 April 2022 as part of his Marine unit. From the moment I met Raf, he was always there for me: helping, teaching, mentoring, making me laugh, and adoring. He just was.

Sooner or later, we will all be gone, and this is the only thing in the human world that cannot be denied. The war makes it no longer scary, but I don't want to do it here and now. Someday I will be glad to see Raf. I'd be glad to see Oleksiy Buslayev in that place that everyone is talking about, but no one knows where it is. Just not today, please.

Oleksiy was right there from the very beginning, through the war and my journey in business after demobilization. He swore like hell and listened to disgusting Russian chanson, which these days can get you a good deal in a very bad district of Kyiv. I wondered how Oleksiy could listen to such music, knowing that he was shooting with a machine gun not only at Donbas separatists, but also at Russians.

I wondered how he decided to fight in the first place. He had his petrol station chain, family, and children. He was rich and at the same time a bright man with no military experience. No necessary skills, but he had iron balls. Everything in his life worked like a Swiss watch. Why did he consciously risk leaving home and not returning, and ultimately never did? What external force drove him there?

He had no ambition, no arrogance. I wanted to be like him, and although I have a lot of complexes and ambition, I am convinced that it appears only when we use these complexes to our advantage.

Oleksiy was killed at war in February 2015. Sometimes I visit him and our guys at the Forest Cemetery in Kyiv. A person lives as long as they are remembered.

Chapter 20

98 Per Cent

This is the story of Mykhailo Vershynin, head of the patrol police in Donetsk region. After being wounded in Mariupol, Mykhailo was evacuated to a hospital in Azovstal, where he joined the garrison's defence. The defence of Azovstal lasted until 20 May 2022, after which Mikhailo survived 123 days of Russian captivity in the Olenivka colony and Donetsk detention centre (SIZO). On 21 September 2022, Ukraine released 215 Azovstal defenders from Russian captivity, including Mikhailo. During that exchange, Russia received only one person – Putin's godfather, Viktor Medvedchuk.

At first, they screamed and pulled the bolts. Then they saw people who had died many times before, and it stopped. The Dagestanis were less aggressive than the Russians. Maybe they were not that humane, but they just had a good memory. For them, we are the ones fighting against yesterday's enslavers of their homeland.

They accompanied us on the way from Azovstal to the Olenivka prison camp and gave us cigarettes and snacks. When the bus stopped, we were allowed to go outside and smoke, but people collapsed after just one cigarette. In Azovstal there was an extreme shortage of tobacco and food.

We were transported all day and night, during which time my mind sank into the abyss and I only came out when the bus pulled up to the gates of the Olenivka detention centre. The convoy was visible from the windows. Burly guards ran behind the prisoners, driving them with sticks.

They organized a raid and took almost everything we had. Barrack 7/8, where I was taken, was designed for 200 people, and there were 604 of us. Mattresses were scattered in the middle of the barrack. There was no water and only one toilet for all the people.

The Russians did not surprise me. They know how to create conditions in which a man and a citizen are in danger of becoming a walking stomach. There was very little food, and what we were given could hardly be called food. Breakfast consisted of a microscopic piece of bread and muesli with glimpses of chicken innards, and tea. No sugar, of course. After breakfast there was an interrogation. Lunch was 'vegetable tea' – water in which vegetables had been boiled, covered with a thin layer of unknown fat. If you were lucky, there were a few pieces of carrot and potato. If the vegetable tea is red, there might be chopped beets floating in it. If the water is muddy and transparent, you might catch old, boiled cabbage. In the afternoon there was another interrogation. Dinner was again bland porridge, sparingly topped with strips of unknown fish. Compared to everything else, at least it was edible.

Constant interrogations. Fingerprints. The Investigative Committee, the FSB, Russian counterintelligence, and the MGS of the DPR. DNA tests, nasal swabs, fingerprints, sophisticated equipment for experiments...

Between interrogations, people split into groups and looked for something to do to keep them from going crazy. They told each other how their moms used to cook borshch. They talked about recipes for various dishes as enthusiastically as if it were the most important thing in life. They did physical exercises with all the strength they had after the meagre diet – there were iron bars in the yard between the barracks for sports. We read books: in the barracks, you could find the *Bible*, collections of short stories, and even the pulp novel *Queen Margot*. Books were a real scarcity. You could not leave them anywhere else – they could be taken away, and then you had to look for them all over the barracks.

There was a territorial defence officer in my barrack. He felt very bad about everything that was happening around him. In civilian life, he was a yoga coach. I asked him to give us a class. Some of us had back pain, some were wounded, and some brains were melting down. Exhausted and powerless, we went outside and tried to repeat the asanas. The *vertukhays* (prison guards) looked at us as if we were aliens. Over time, some of us stopped having severe pain, some started sleeping better, and some calmed down.

It is impossible to tame the mind without taming the body. I used to get up at 4.30 am every morning when it was still dark. I did a series of physical exercises: push-ups, squats, press-ups. The fence in Olenivka is painted with my marks of the days and approaches. I would take a nail and scratch marks on it with my sports performance. After sports, I would go to the flooded cellar to fetch water, fill a canister, and douse myself. In the beginning we had soap and towels to keep us relatively clean.

All this allowed you to start the day knowing that you were still alive and had every chance of carrying on. To do that, you had to find something that allowed you not to slip into an animal state. What do you have when you own nothing? Only what is inside you.

One guy was left with a phone during the shakedown at the entrance to Olenivka – maybe that's how they wanted to keep an eye on us. He helped me write messages to my family. I gave him a piece of paper on which I wrote what I wanted to say. 'My Bunnies'. I call my family 'My Bunnies'. 'I'm fine, I love you, and I miss you very much.'

At midnight, he would type the text on his phone and could send it within a very short period because the Russians jammed the communication with electronic warfare. The next day he came to me, blushing. He said, 'Read this, you'll be pleased', and handed me a piece of paper with the answer.

At first, I carried these pieces of paper with me, but then the big shakedowns started, and I had to destroy them. It's good that this guy has already been released from captivity; he works for the Lviv patrol police now.

My comrades in captivity and I used to organize rituals with small human joys. After dinner we would kneel and share an extra piece or two of bread that some of us had received. We would brew a cup of tea and drink it in small sips. If it had sugar in it, it was a real feast. Sugar, salt, tea, and cigarettes were the local currency.

We shared everything we had. The fact that you were not alone and that you were sharing something delicious with people made me feel very good and warm inside.

We would squat down in a circle, light a cigarette, and take turns taking a drag. When you stand up abruptly afterward, it's getting dark in your eyes, and you feel dizzy. It's enough to make thoughts go quiet for a moment.

No one in our company smoked alone, as other people usually did when they locked themselves in the toilet. It is the only place where you can be alone, and there is always a queue. Everyone has digestive problems due to malnutrition and poor hygiene. Sometimes guys would come out of the toilet wobbly, and their gaze looking like fish eyes. One cigarette takes your head away and makes the whole body shake if you don't smoke and are malnourished.

Sooner or later, each of us will find a place in our souls for everything that was in captivity. And we will remember these moments of small human joy as the best thing that happened on another terrible day with no hope for the future. We will be glad that we did not fall apart. You can be a valiant warrior but break down and lose yourself. Learn to wag your tail in front of the *vertukhays* for the sake of double rations. In addition to those loyal to the leadership, it was also given to those who did some dirty work. For example, removing waste from a constantly clogged toilet and taking it all outside the barracks.

One day, while lining up, one of the guys decided to tempt fate and shouted the phrase 'Glory to Ukraine'. He was answered by the rest of the line with the response 'Glory to the heroes'. The next day it happened again. On the third day, the cry of 'Glory to the heroes' was picked up by many people. After that, Volyna[11] – the block elder in our barracks – was taken to the punishment cell for twenty-eight days.

I was called for another interrogation. The prison owner (so-called Kum in every jail), said, 'Your Volyna doesn't know the ropes. One of the guards reported that Volyna was collecting money in the barracks to give to him to buy cigarettes for the prisoners.' As a former criminal investigation officer, he was outraged.

From time to time, the guys saw Volyna in pieces – he was beaten to a pulp and was walking black and blue.

When I was transferred to the Donetsk detention centre in mid-July, I was able to do 300 push-ups from the floor. My arm recovered a bit after the injury. The Olenivka barracks, with its 'honourable captivity' on the floor with mattresses, seemed like a sanatorium compared to the place where I later ended up. There I met men from the 501st Brigade, with whom we held Mariupol for a while. Their commander had ordered them to lay down their arms, and in captivity they sincerely regretted not dying on the battlefield.

The cell is three by seven (10 by 23 feet). Ten beds for twenty-five people. Toilet in public, washing in public, and it's good if you can somehow wash twice a week; 150 grams (5 ounces) of water with mud per person. It's either hellishly hot or terribly cold, with no in-between. A narrow window overlooking a concrete fence, a bush and a small patch of sky. No walks. Lice. Bedbugs. Beatings.

If the camera doesn't do as it's told, the special forces run in and beat anything they can reach with sticks. And God forbid someone didn't have time to fall face first to the floor when they entered the cell.

I took great care of the gold cross on a necklace my mother gave me. I even hid it in my mouth so they wouldn't take it away.

The *vertukhay* who took me to the next interrogation saw me adjusting something on my right shoulder – it was hidden there. He searched me and took the cross away.

I couldn't sleep near anyone, so I just lay down on the cold concrete, which made me very sick. A man from our cell, a little over 20 years old, burned to death in a few days – no help was given to him. I thought about his fate and that his family would never know how he was. And I realized that I was unlikely to get out of there myself. The chances of an exchange are slim. My family will never know where I ended up, what happened to me, where I was buried.

I didn't believe in anything good, even when they took us out and read out our personal files and accused us of taking up arms again. It's very Russian to give hope and then take it away. Then give it back and take it away. Again, and again – until the person burns out from the inside. This is a different kind of torture. Even before the full-scale invasion, they would often take prisoners to the contact line and talk about an exchange. Then they would put them in a vehicle and say that Ukraine had abandoned them. The aim is to make people believe that nobody needs them. After three or four such trips in a row, a person will unconsciously perceive his state as hostile.

Every hour I assessed the situation and gave it a percentage of optimism. They took us out of the cell and put us on a bus: there was a 50 per cent chance of an exchange. We were taken somewhere in an unknown direction: 20 per cent. They take us somewhere, and it's quiet around us, and by all accounts it could be Vasylivka, and sometimes they do exchanges there: 70 per cent chance. They take us on a long and boring journey without food and water, and my internal barometer shows 30 per cent.

One moment I didn't believe in anything, the next I was starting my life from scratch. Then I would give up and hope for an exchange.

They put us on a cargo plane and it's a fiasco. They will take us somewhere and we will stay there for the rest of our lives. That is no more than 10 per cent.

The day after we left the cells, a man came on the bus and started saying our names.

'Vershynin!'

My name sounded Ukrainian. I got up and headed for the exit.

'Say something else in Ukrainian', I asked in a whisper as I passed him.

'Glory to Ukraine', he said very quietly.

'Glory to the heroes.'

There, it was 98 per cent. I was still afraid that this was another Russian performance.

At the exit of the bus there were two tall, rude Russians. They took the ties off my hands and I walked forward.

It was cold outside, and I was only wearing a T-shirt. It's still warm in the east of Ukraine at this time of year, so it must be up north. A man caught up with me and gave me a fleece jacket. He said, 'Here, I have one more...' I put it on. It was a bit warmer, so I walked on. There were people on both sides. I was afraid that one of my chiefs from the police would be there. My eyesight is not good, it would be very embarrassing to walk past. My face was wet from frontal sinusitis, genyantritis, and conjunctivitis, and I was afraid to approach people. The closer you get to their faces, the more you see their pitying looks, and I hate pity. As long as I don't see the face of the nurse giving me a shot of anaesthetic, I'm fine. But when I see her tears, I feel sick. I don't understand why she's crying and what's wrong with me. But then, for the first time in months, I looked in the mirror at my sloping face with sharp cheekbones and realized why they were looking at me like that and why that nurse was crying.

They gave me a bottle of water with lemon, Napoleon biscuits, and some cigarettes. Some of the boys jumped on the biscuits and they were gone in no time. I went and got some more. We chewed the biscuits and smoked with pleasure. I found a telephone somewhere and called my family. They put us back on the buses and drove us away.

The doctors told me that if I had stayed in captivity another two days with my illness, I would not have come back...

That first night I could not sleep for a long time. I walked around the hospital room, touching the bedside tables, the fridge, and the door handles.

The day after my return was 22 September, my birthday. I owe God a lot. I owe him for everything I learned in captivity. I owe him that birthday and every day since.

I still cannot come out of captivity when hundreds of our people are there. I walk the streets of a beautiful city and it makes me uncomfortable. Every time I eat, I think of those who are now hungry. When I go to bed, I think of those lying on the concrete. When I talk to my family, I think of those who do not have the same opportunities and do not know if they will ever see their loved ones again.

And yet, when my day is over, I talk to God and think about the fact that I lived it exactly the way I was supposed to. I did what I wanted to do, and I was useful.

But I am not free. I'm 98 per cent out of captivity. I will be released only together with the last person who was captured by Russia and lived this ordeal nobly.

Chapter 21

WHAT HAPPENED TO THAT GRANDPA

Narrator Denys Kobzin is a director of the Kharkiv Institute for Social Research and human rights activist. Denys's story continues the reinterpretation of his combat experience, after which he was involved in a group to overcome combat stress. Denys helps other combatants overcome the psychological challenges of war.

I have been on other operations in the Kharkiv region, including in the same village of Ruska Lozova. We drove the Russians away from there as far as the village of Prokhody, and they could no longer fire on Kharkiv so closely. However, none of these operations returned to my mind for months after I got out of there alive.

During combat stress, the amygdala, which is responsible for instincts and survival, is activated. Instead, the brain's frontal lobe is supposed to 'produce' empathy, informed decisions, and pleasure. Almost a year has passed, and it is still difficult to talk about anything other than the war. I used to be a film buff, but for many months I stopped keeping up. I couldn't listen to music for a long time.

I almost lost contact with people who did not have military experience. I don't respond to messages from people who fell through the ground on 24 February and then suddenly became interested in how I am. It's like clothes you have already grown out of, even though you wore them many years before: everyone remembers you as you were before, but now you are not the same.

Once, the guys I lived with were taken away at night for some military operation. I found out in the morning when I woke up alone in the room.

As soon as they were placed at the observation post, everything went up in flames. All kinds of weapons were working, a fighter plane flew overhead, and everyone was running away under fire. One guy also ran away but suddenly remembered the thermal imager, returned for it, and only then left the position.

A day later, two of them returned with all the signs of shell shock.

Somebody called guys to the company commander, who did not hear anyone and called them deserters. The guy with the thermal imager couldn't find a place to sit and kept repeating, 'I'm a deserter; I'll be shot.' I tried to talk to him, but there was no point – he was looking not at the world but through it.

I am convinced that people with similar experiences should work with the military after combat stress. It is easy for me to find a common language with a person who has been under mortar fire – no matter how long we have known each other. With those who have survived combat operations, we understand each other at a glance. It seems to me that I can help people who are on the edge of the abyss precisely because we have similar experiences. We have similar situations and similar characters around us. We are equally vulnerable. We recognize each other instantly, and I still don't understand external signs. We know where to laugh and where to frown during a conversation.

In my practice, there were two cases close to suicide.

One guy was left by his wife. They had two children and a house. This guy was a builder by profession, and he built the house himself. His wife went abroad and told him that she would not return home to him. This is a typical case in the circumstances of Ukrainian families, but for this man, his home and family were everything. The walls of his house were crumbling, like the same ravaged house outside of which I held the chief on my shoulders to shoot back with a sniper rifle. It turned into a mountain of building materials as if there had never been any family comfort there.

Another one was very broken after the death of his comrade. We take the deaths of our comrades-in-arms very hard. Not long after that, his mother died. In his life outside the frontline, it was the only umbilical cord that connected him to life, and he planned to end it.

When we are holding the defence together, we constantly think of our families, but when we return home or even on leave, we cannot forgive ourselves for leaving our comrades. It was easier for me because I was constantly in circumstances where I didn't know anyone. These people did not have time to become my family. I didn't know anything about the people I knew.

There was a guy called Cat who lived with me. We mainly met during sleepovers and never participated in the same operations. I don't even know his real name. I don't know who he was before the war. In all the photos, he is wearing a balaclava or turning away from the camera. I wouldn't be surprised if Cat had a criminal past – his manners somewhat resembled the behaviour of a petty criminal. However, it was good to live with him and talk about topical issues. He's a very humane guy, and I hope he's still alive – whatever his past was before he joined the army.

After all, I am a stranger everywhere myself. Sometimes I remember a conversation with the owner of that red-roofed house in the village of Ruska Lozova. We were standing in the backyard and smoking.

'This alabai dog is a real miracle. The children love him very much, and so does everyone who comes to our house. He is very playful, he needs attention all the time, and that's why the house is always noisy and joyful', the man said.

'I thought it was so good that he didn't see who was aiming at their pet: I was wearing a balaclava at the time.'

Perhaps I would not have been able to help these people who wanted to commit suicide if it hadn't been for that incident with

Prosecutor. He asked the two guys he lived with to leave the room, and then shot himself.

Prosecutor was a very witty and charismatic man, but his sense of humour was a small bridge over the abyss. Humour helps the military survive, but his chasm must have been so wide and deep and his bridge so thin and fragile that he could not balance from one end to the other.

Ultimately, the only thing you can control when you have no control over your life is the fact of it.

When the full-scale war started, I completely lost control of my life. I used to have everything. I felt like I was at the helm of my ship. But at one point, it all disappeared. A storm started in my sea, and I began to drown amid the elements, where I had no control over anything and no influence on anything.

Of course, when the Russians came to Kharkiv, we all became outraged. Ordinary people on the street, who had never thought about the country's fate, wanted to fight those who came to their homes without permission. They wanted revenge for their broken home, neighbourhood, and hometown. There is no worse feeling than when everything around you is on fire, and you have bare hands, and you can't do anything about it. Everyone wanted to fight back against the bastards, to take the enemy by the throat with one hand and hold the steering wheel with the other.

I still haven't regained my sense of control. In the army, this is difficult by default – this is how the whole institution works. It is even more complicated when you once had it and suddenly lost it. And I try to do everything I can to feel the steering wheel of my life, at least by touch.

When lunchtime comes, I don't go to the canteen with my colleagues. I go to the shop and buy a salad or a roll. This way, I have an additional opportunity to control my own life. And it comes back to me whenever I help others find a place in their minds for everything they have experienced.

If you do not find a place for this in your own experience and do not look at yourself from the outside, these things will haunt you for as long as you want and hurt you. You will find yourself back in that dugout again, being carried from side to side by the shock wave. Your body will release the same adrenaline as it did then, making your mouth dry. You will dream about the voice of a company officer dying from the shrapnel that got under his vest.

But I have an almost healing memory from there that still helps me fight insomnia. I still remember the heaviness of my own eyelids when Grandpa and I returned from duty and wanted to take a nap before the National Guard replaced us. I laid down and leaned my head against something, and it was one of the most pleasant sensations a human body can have. My eyelids felt like bags of cement. When I can't sleep, I remember those twenty minutes of bliss with my eyes closed.

My return from that battle was painful and prolonged. Thank God, I came back. My unit commander said he saw the checkpoint where I came under the heaviest fire in my life from a neighbouring position. No one was waiting for me after three days without communication.

'We thought no one would survive there – everything was smoking and flying in the air', he says.

When I returned to Kharkiv, I was utterly exhausted and met my unit commander to talk about everything that had happened. Suddenly, Grandpa came into the room. He and a few other guys went to another checkpoint and got to the evacuation point a few hours earlier.

I started crying. I thought Grandpa was dead. He thought I was dead. We sat down and cried together.

Chapter 22

LITTLE BERTHA

The narrator of this story is Oleksiy Dytrykh, a sapper with the call sign Gunter. Oleksiy tells about the events of 2017–2018 during the Joint Forces Operation in Donbas. Gunter was the name of Oleksiy's grandfather, the German who took part in the Second World War as part of the SS Viking Panzer Division and was captured at the Kursk Bulge. During the capture, he was involved in reconstructing the Ukrainian city of Kharkiv and met Oleksiy's grandmother, a Ukrainian woman. After Stalin's death, he did not return to Germany, as his village was destroyed. He built a house in Transnistria and worked as a carpenter.

Little Bertha's story began in a mined garage full of ammunition. If you put your head through the gate, you'd get a small nuclear blast. To clear this garage, I had to lift a piece of slate. I carefully pushed it aside and dove inside.

There was a wire attached to the garage door and a grenade on the other side of the wire. The enemy was leaving and had no time to take everything with them. They decided to surprise us with all this stuff in the garage and mined it. In Shyrokyne, we lived with the combat medics in the three-storey house opposite. It would have collapsed like a house of cards in such an explosion.

There was a vast quantity of ammunition, and our entire command came to see this treasure. But we had no way to use these mines and shells.

'Gunther, we must make something for this calibre ourselves. Sniper Fix showed how the Syrians make guns out of whatever they have at hand', said Arkasha, my good friend and comrade-in-arms.

'What are you going to do, bro?'

'It would be great to find a metal pipe to match the calibre and pour their ammo back at them.'

We were warned that artillery cadets would come from Russia to take their exams. The reconnaissance told us that Shyrokyne was going to be wiped off the map with artillery coming from the village of Sakhanka.

So Little Bertha was destined to be born out of anything, even shit and sticks.

I remembered the bastion position. This is a two-storey house almost on the edge of Shyrokyne, not far from the enemy trenches. The roof was completely smashed, but there was a good basement where we kept machine guns. The road to the bastion was shelled and covered with mine holes.

We took some ammunition from the garage and went to the bastion. There was a solid gate in front of the building which was supported by a thick stainless-steel pipe. We wanted to push an 82-calibre mine inside the pipe, but it didn't work. However, an liquefied natural gas (LNG) shell fit well.

We blew up the gate with a detonating cord: the pipe was concreted, and the gate could not be removed from its hinges because of the welded corners – maybe the owner was afraid that one day his gate would be sold for scrap metal. The house used to belong to one of the local police chiefs, but he left for the Russian city of Rostov-on-Don when the hostilities started.

Arkasha and I were dragging the gate with the pipe to our house, and the commander of the second Marine company, call sign Count, was standing outside and taking a long drag on his cigarette.

'Hey, looters! Where are you taking the gate?'

'It will be a cannon or a mortar.'

The Count twirled his finger at his temple, and we dragged the gate further to our position, sawed it off with the generator, and took it to the garden and summer kitchen. There used to be a water well there. The pump is gone, and the source is silted up, but there was a piece of rail to which it was all attached.

We taped our pipe to this rail. We found 60 metres (200 feet) of internet cable somewhere in the bins. I also had my undermining machine, which I made myself from everything I found in abandoned buildings in Shyrokyne and at the market in Mariupol.

As expected, we were shelled from the Sakhansk bulge. The cadets were warming up with the 120 mortar and preparing the artillery. The basement, where we were waiting, was moving, but there were no orders.

'Arkasha, our turn.'

'We can be punished for this. Unauthorized firing.'

'They'll reload now. There will be a massive shelling, and we'll be shooting for the noise.'

'We need to shoot at something, not just anything! What are we going to say? That we have moulded *Wunderwaffe* here? They won't let us do that.'

'Who's going to look for that? Let's go…'

We went outside and turned the pipe towards the Sakhanka bulge, from where the enemy was shelling Shyrokyne. We loaded the pipe with an LNG rocket and crouched under a summer kitchen with a blasting machine. I pulled the trigger.

The sound of the explosion was so abominable that we almost fainted. I wanted to bury myself in the ground. LNG fires in a completely different way and does not have such a whistle.

A little further behind the bastion, there was the ranch position from above. This is a former recreation centre with a bathhouse and swimming pool – it used to belong to some official. Elf, a Marine sniper, was sitting there.

'Wonderful! Now, twenty to the left', Elf's voice came over the radio.

So, we didn't know what twenty is, but over there to the left! We moved our pipe a little bit with our foot and charged it again.

The shells we launched flew over the trenches with our comrades and went on to the Russians. No one from our side understood what was shooting and where it was coming from. It was impossible to determine the type of weapon. Such vile sounds hardly existed in nature before that moment.

Arkasha and I fired two more shells, and the shelling from the other side stopped at once.

In the evening, Arkasha and I went to the 'office' – that's what everyone called the meeting house, where everyone talks, drinks coffee with cookies and condensed milk, smokes, and exchanges news.

We lay low and eavesdropped. Our commander, call sign June, was declared as a star today.

'You guys are so handsome! You saved the day. They were really scared there.'

Commander June stood there like a stone and did not understand anything.

'But we didn't shoot... We thought it was you who were shooting from your control and observation point.'

'Hell, we have two Ural trucks and a Hummer burnt. The strikes were clearly from the 'Alice' position', said Maradona, the Marines' deputy commander.

'Alice' is the house where Arkasha and I live with the medics. Everyone around fell silent.

'I know who that was', Count broke in. 'Recently, two crazy looters were dragging a stainless-steel gate here. I asked them where they were putting it. They said they were going to make a cannon. I thought the guys were badly shell-shocked...'

Seemed like we were done, but the commanders showed us the radio intercept data. We hit the house where the enemy headquarters was located with this pipe. At that very moment, the artillery command was planning that massive shelling of Shyrokyne our reconnaissance informed us about. Eleven Russian officers were killed and eight were seriously wounded.

'You're dead, boys! The 'DPR' police are looking for you! They think the Americans have entered Shyrokyne and that we have Abrams here…'

People came to our Alice from all positions like pilgrims to look at where the enemy command headquarters had been smashed from. People stood over a bent pipe taped to the rail and laughed at the top of their lungs.

Arkasha and I received an order.

'Get the cannon and these two to the Green position on the left flank. We are to bring them ammo if necessary. Let them work on Sakhanka day and night!'

We were as happy as little children and decided to modify our design. Volunteers brought us a welding machine. We came across an upside-down burnt-out 'ant hill' scooter. We took off the body and cut off the back. Our gun had a wheelbase. The lift was now regulated by a jack from an old Zhiguli car.

Arkasha asked what to call our creation. I named her Little Bertha.

My dog Mira was excited to fraternize with Little Bertha. She liked to pull the cannon on wheels down the hill at the Green. We tied a baby carriage loaded with shells to Little Bertha. Mira was in the front of the harness.

One day, Arkasha, Mira, and I were dragging ourselves up the street to shoot at the Green and saw two civilian jeeps. On the side stood our Count, a girl in a helmet and bulletproof vest with the word 'PRESS', and a guy with a video camera.

'What's this? Is this the legendary Bertha?'

'No, don't pay attention to that...' said Count and grabbed his head, shamed.

The reporters surrounded us. Little Bertha became a mini celebrity. She toured Donbas with us. Once during rotation, Arkasha and I brought her home to my friend Pavlo in Mariupol.

'Don't worry', I said, 'it's not asking for food. We'll take it all in detail now.'

'Are you mad? Tomorrow they'll come for me! It's a weapon!'

Little Bertha's golden hour came in Vodyane near Donetsk. Pavlo took her details to the Post Office. He told them he was sending a motorized plow and a pipe for a stove. The pipe weighed 40 kilograms (90 pounds). Of course, no one believed him.

Once we wanted to make another mortar for the 120th mortar. On the Novoazovsk Road between the bastion and the green, we spotted a wrecked enemy tank with a 125-calibre muzzle. This tank used to come here from Sakhanka, break down the wall of a house or farm, and shoot at us from the windows. The Nazis did this during the Second World War. For a long time, we couldn't understand where the shots were coming from.

The tank was hit by a guy from our battalion, call sign Lens, a typical IT guy with glasses who had nothing to do with the army until 2014. It was a matter of honour for him. After his friend Mole was halved by an unexploded shell in this tank, Lens hunted him down day and night. Other guys came to take over, but Lens waited long and tediously for this tank and finally got his revenge.

The tank was full of ammo and fuel: they had left for a long time and took everything with them so as not to return to Sakhanka for diesel. The explosion of all this was so powerful that it tore off the muzzle tower.

Not far from here was an enemy position we called Star. There were five of us: sniper Elf, Arkasha, me, a Marine sapper in about his fiftieth Serhiyovych. And there was a guy named Speed Racer.

'Guys, I want to go with you!'

'Speed Racer, why do you want to? They're going to start shooting from the Star. How are you going to run?'

Speed Racer is the call sign of a guy who had one leg. I don't know under what circumstances he lost it, but it was before the war. Volunteers brought him a prosthetic leg, and now he was rushing to go to fight with us.

We wrapped a detonating cord between the turret and the muzzle, but for such a design, it was nothing more than a shock to the air. We put a box of TNT and two anti-tank mines inside. When the time came to blow it all up, I noticed that Serhiyovych had left only 5 centimetres (2 inches) of cord to set it on fire.

No wonder he was sometimes called Maniac. Tall, bald, in his glasses, he somewhat resembled the maniac Chikatilo. There is a story with him in the main part about how he asked volunteers to find him a Russian uniform. He changed clothes, went to those bastards at night, and got drunk with them. While hanging out with them, Serhiyovych stuck mines right into their trenches. When the explosion started, Serhiyovych had already run away from them. The next day, he drew us a complete diagram of their trenches, told us where he was, how many people were there, when they made exchanges, where the firing points were, how many, and what kind of equipment – we knew everything.

'Why are you squeezing? Make more cord', I said.

'Guys', Serhiyovych said, 'This is so you can learn to run fast.'

Serhiyovych lit the fire, and we all took off running. The Elf and Arkasha picked up speed, and I was a little behind. I looked back and saw Serhiyovych running too. Serhiyovych is a 2 metre (6.5 foot)-tall man. His one step is as long as our ten. It seemed that he would leap over us all like an ostrich and be the only one to survive this adventure. I was laughing until I cried, and I seemed to slow down.

And then I saw Speed Racer overtaking me on his prosthetic leg, and my stomach started to tear up from laughter. I thought, what the hell, the enemy saw all this. They saw us putting something in the tower, running away, saw this furious explosion – and they didn't even shoot.

At one point, we all fell to the ground. The Elf said he saw the tower make two turns in the air and hit the asphalt 0.5 metre away. It seemed that it was not a part of the tank that exploded, but the whole world. We made our way through the smoke to the turret, which was blown open like a flower. The muzzle was stuck in the ground but did not come off.

'Boys, it's time to dump, now they will start pouring…'

And as soon as we reached the bastion, they started to shoot. We ran under fire again and laughed like crazy. And then we laughed again, told all this to others so that they would laugh too.

We never made the 120th mortar. Our commander June received somehow the 'Hero of Ukraine' award. (Arkasha and I weren't counting on any regalia anyway.) Mykhailo Kravchuk, call sign Arkasha, my friend and helper who understood me implicitly, died during the full-scale invasion. Commander June is also gone. Serhiyovych was discharged even before the full-scale war began.

The first Abrams tanks in Ukraine will appear in six years from that time. Little Bertha remained unique and unrepeatable.

Chapter 23

NEW YORK[12]

Narrator Hryhoriy Dekhtyar is lieutenant colonel of the Armed Forces of Ukraine, battalion commander of the mechanized battalion of the 30th Separate Mechanized Brigade. He has been participating in the Russian-Ukrainian war since the defence of Crimea in 2014.

My father committed suicide when I was too small to remember it. When I grew up, my mother finally stopped coming back home. I played truant in computer clubs, had Ds in school, and lived alone since I was 10 years old in the part of the house that belonged to my mother. My aunt, her sister, lived next door. Sometimes she would come to visit me to check if I was alive. Then I accidentally got into the Bohun Military School in Kyiv. I saw it all, and I wanted to live it.

Some say the army is for the brave, but in reality, it is more suitable for the lazy. If you cannot or don't want to take care of yourself, someone will come along and push you to do so. If you don't know how to do something, someone will tell you and show you how to do it. If you have no sense of purpose in life, someone will quickly come up with one for you. You are clothed, fed, and paid. Figuratively, you have no problems with sex in the army! You get f*cked every day...

Semen (Anatoliy Semenenko), our company commander, always advised us to work on ourselves. He would say, 'Commander, you should learn a lot.' In many ways, I wanted to be like him and realized how important it was.

In 2022, Vitalik, a commander of the 25th Brigade and my fellow neighbour on the right in the New York defence, entered the military university with me. He studied part-time, and I studied full-time. When his brigade was transferred to Bakhmut, I had to order and send him three Mavic mounts. I promised to do the whole thing in a week, but they arrived later. I thought he was offended as he didn't read my messages for several days. I was about to call him. At night, I received a text saying that he and two of his soldiers had been killed by shells.

New York, formerly Troitske, especially teaches you what the price of life is. Nothing gives such an understanding of the value of it as an evacuation stretcher.

They say that the best and most professional people are those who die in war. Bullshit. The most active ones die.

You can stand idly by the whole war and come back with a bunch of medals. Or you can constantly move around, shoot, put yourself in danger, and not return home at all. Or not return because of ridiculous decisions from above, like Semen. Semen did not believe in his mortality so much that he jokingly asked to choose a good photo for his obituary.

Why would he die? He has a wife, and two kids, is almost 2 metres (6.5 foot) tall, speaks fluent English, studied in the United States, attended officer training courses and veteran soccer tournaments, and served a mission in Kosovo twice. He has orders, medals, and awards. He always has tea, coffee, sandwiches, and cookies for everyone who visits him. When people came to him on business or just for fun, it made him happy. He only knew how to live.

He died on 19 September 2022, in the Donetsk region. It is not clear why he was ordered to go to that forest, and for what purpose two of our groups devoted their lives. Several people were sent for Semen's body, and none of them returned.

Perhaps those who sent him to that forest pretentiously call Semen a hero, because he died for his country. But he, an experienced military man, would hardly think so. A good commander – he was that one and remains in our memory – does not want to be a hero. Moreover, he does not need heroes among his personnel.

We came to the New York position with a staffing level of 99 per cent, and four months later we were at 97 per cent: fourteen killed, sixty-one wounded, thirty of whom returned to combat missions. The guys mobilized in February 2022 reached the combat level of contractors with experience in Congo and Kosovo in six months.

I'm proud of these people and I keep telling them that. People need to feel important in war. And it's not heroism and initiative that should make them important, but another person: the commander. A man in a trench is particularly vulnerable because he does not have a complete picture of what is happening around him. In the trench, you can see 300 to 400 shells of cannon artillery and air bombs flying in your direction, and you can't see the end of it. As a commander, I must constantly talk about their successes, like how they destroyed an enemy depot, hit a Russian tank, and neutralized a whole group. I must find words that inspire a person to stay in position for another week, two weeks, or a month.

In May 2022, during the full-scale invasion, it happened that nine guys from my battalion stopped the assault on their own, which meant about seventy infantry units, two tanks, and an infantry fighting vehicle. Then they were sent reinforcements, but this repulsion of the assault remained their triumph.

This, but not heroism, is always inspiring. Your feat will not necessarily inspire others. Losses always affect the morale and psychological state of a person at war. When 1,000 shells hit every day for two weeks, but there are ten to twenty dead and ten to fifteen wounded, people perceive losses normally. They do not see themselves so clearly on tomorrow's list. They are ready to stand on.

But when forty comrades are killed in two hours of fighting, the one stops believing that one day he will return home and hug his wife and children. He asks himself why and for what purpose he should die here, in New York, and not in old age by the fireplace.

However, it is easier to work with hesitation than with a person's desire to be a hero. There is no need to fight for a position if it is not of strategic importance. Look around and think about what prevented you from creating the conditions to avoid fighting for it. Because when you win it back at a high cost, it may turn out that this position is not so important that you need to use the reserve there. Because when you win it back at the cost of dozens and hundreds of human lives, you will have to ask yourself.

Why did you give that order?

Why did people die?

Why was the 25th Brigade ordered to enter a wooded area where the men were torn apart?

When the 25th Brigade was replaced by the 110th Brigade near New York, we offered any help we could. We have drones, we can see everything here, we can detect everything. The main thing is just to stay here, don't panic, and don't run away.

The third cock hadn't sung when their commander said, 'We've been breached, I'm retreating.' I looked at him. All his men were standing, no one was running away. Only one enemy tank was a kilometre away lazily puffing in the direction of their control and observation post. I warned them about this tank as soon as they got to the position that we should ambush it, hit it, and forget about it. But suddenly, everyone started running away from there. Their commander didn't even stay in that position for half a day.

'Guys, people are coming, they are ours, don't shoot at them', I told my people.

We heard shots.

'They are ours, I told you not to shoot!'

'I'm not shooting at them. I'm only shooting in that direction so that they don't run away.'

'Why?'

'Where are they all running to? There are so many of them!'

'But they don't know who their commander is...'

That is why I tend to think that the Russians blew up the Crimean Bridge themselves. It is logical.

The commander who fled gave up a Starlink, batteries for a third Mavic, and three Rapiers there. For weeks I was going around asking people whose Rapiers were there, trying to get them back. We could shoot a lot with them while repelling four assaults in a day. But the owner was not found, and the enemy came to those positions and shot at us with those Rapiers.

It's illogical to create conditions for the enemy in which they cannot escape. It is even dangerous to surround the enemy. Azovstal fought to the last, and this inspired hundreds and thousands of soldiers to fight. That's why it's easier to fight against the Russians, even with their powerful artillery and aviation, than against the Donbas separatists. The separatists had a goal and nowhere to retreat. And that is why Russians were desperately fleeing from the Kharkiv direction. Everything was alien to them there, and there was nowhere to go.

When there is nowhere to run, people start to be themselves. Azovstal was born in a place with no options.

I remember how it feels when there are no options.

In 2015, we organized a raid 1,000 kilometres (620 miles) behind enemy lines to cut off their supplies. I was then with the 95th Brigade between Krasnyi Luch and Anthracite. The distance between the companies was about 10 kilometres (6 miles). Our first company was the farthest away. There were no longer 100 people in each company, as it should be. In some companies, there were only two dozen men, and they fought like that.

We stopped at a crossroads and realized it was a trap. There was nowhere to go further and nowhere to go back.

The separatists knew we were there. Their scouts saw us and our tanks. We had two tanks, and only one was in working condition.

We put it right on the road and pointed the gun in the direction of the enemy.

They were shouting at us to surrender knowing that there was nowhere to go for us. It looked like the beginning of the end. We shot back a little, but it didn't help. They shouted again and again.

'Surrender, Mr Trenin', somebody said. They knew the name of our commander.

It is unclear how many of them were there, hundreds or thousands. But there were four dozen of us.

They took the commander but let him go after an hour and a half. He started calling his family. He called everyone else to surrender.

'There is no chance anyway, and there they do not beat, mock, or torture. We must surrender...', he said. Part of the company was relatively weak and agreed to this.

Fear mobilizes and provides additional resources. Hopelessness can also be controlled. In fact, it is nothing that eats a person from the inside, but panic. Panic spreads like a cancer metastasizing throughout the body.

I wanted to shoot him on the spot myself, I really mean it. It seemed as if I was the bigger enemy because I did not let him raise the white flag.

My unit supported me. Reinforcements were promised to arrive soon. We were partially saved by the fact that the enemy did not know how few of us there were. They didn't storm us, they just shelled us with artillery. We waited five days. Reinforcements made a 'corridor' for us, and somehow we left. I will remember that road forever.

Chapter 24

FRAGMENTS

The narrator is Anastasia Podobaylo, a paramedic of the 56th Separate Motorized Infantry Brigade. At 18, she entered the faculty of philology at the university in her native city of Kharkiv, but decided to connect her future with military life.

I barely remember if he said anything while handing me the wedding band. Apparently, there was a lack of time to say a word because I didn't let him pronounce anything substantive.

'One way or another, a girl has to accept a gift, even if she refuses.' These are the only words I remember speaking amid my ramblings about how important it was to remain friends.

Not only didn't I remember what he said, but also what I was talking about. What words did I use to bargain with myself? How did I convince myself that we were, first and foremost, comrades? What arguments did I choose to refuse?

Out of six years in this war, he had been with me for two, which is a third of the most conscious period of my life.

That conversation has melted into my memory. Sometimes the wounded don't remember what they are talking about when they come to me on an evacuation stretcher. If the injury is very bad, and the person retains consciousness, they are driven by something incomparable.

The most poignant thing that can come out of the mouth of a seriously wounded person is not screams or pleas for rescue, but the names of their wives, husbands, and everything that is connected with them.

One man of my dad's age with an artery wound under his collarbone was bleeding and calling for his mother. Who knows if she is alive, but this was enough to keep him alive.

Another older man, almost 60 years old, said that he had four children and six grandchildren, and he did not understand why he was there and why the Russians attacked us. He is quite seriously wounded, and I am unsure if he may be able to walk at all.

The hardest thing is to help guys younger than me. I look at an 18-year-old boy who has been weakened by shell fragments or a bullet and see myself, the one who once came here hoping to quickly save the world from universal evil and return to a peaceful life of doing something more creative. In fact, at his age, I was shamefully lucky, and he will have to go on with his life, walking with a prosthesis. I hope he will have one.

Guys who have just recently had a baby and are eager to see it, or are waiting for their wife to give birth, for some unfathomable reason end up on stretchers. At least now when life can be cut short, this is all they can talk about.

Most of the time, people on the verge of death really do remember the people they love. It's the first thing that comes out of their subconscious.

Sometimes they behave in a completely unpredictable way. They don't even let you get to the wound: of course, no one likes to be touched where it hurts the most. And I'm sure they even don't remember their actions. If I jokingly asked them after stabilization something like, 'Dear friend, how do you live with yourself after you took a mouthful of water, spat on me, and definitely wet your pants to prevent me from working?', he would not understand what I meant.

Probably, if I lived every story that fell into my hands, I would have broken down long ago. I carry my own shell fragments inside me, and if I collect other people's along the way, I wouldn't have the strength to heal myself and continue working.

'Yashka, just imagine, I dreamed about you today!'

'Wow, how? Tell me…'

'I dreamed about the war, and you and I were together holding the defence of my native Kharkiv.'

'Holy cow, how cool is that!'

Yashka is a painful fragment in my heart. He was such a bright person that absolutely everything sounded cool from his lips. That conversation took place on 22 February 2022. Two weeks later, I learned that Yashka had disappeared during the defence of Kharkiv. The enemy almost reached the very centre of the city, where my parents live. Yasha's body was found only after the deoccupation of the Kharkiv region.

I am sorry our last conversation was like that. If I could, I would have said completely different words. About how much I love him. And that in his presence, people grow wings. That he is a very good friend. And that thanks to his efforts, in particular, my mom and dad, who remained in Kharkiv, did not know the sorrow of an occupation.

I didn't want to believe it was true, even though it seemed a likely option in the aftermath of a full-scale invasion. My group and I were surrounded not far from Mariupol three times and barely made it out of there. We had four wounded, and I found out about the death of Yashka on the phone on the way to Dnipro, taking the deceased from our unit for an autopsy.

Tengri is another painful fragment in my heart. When Yashka was being buried, my friend Natalka and I went to the grave of our mutual friend, sniper Tengri.

There are legends about who Tengri is. Not a lot of people know his real name. He successfully completed countless difficult and risky missions. A tall and sturdy man with a humble face, always silent, he looked not like a warrior but like a loving husband and father, an intellectual erudite who once lived an ordinary life and went to work at a local history museum in the Poltava region. We became good friends over time, and I'll never forget how tenderly he told me about his first date with his wife. It was almost two decades ago, but he remembered all the details. He must have been an extremely sensitive person to love a woman so much.

When we came to Tengri's grave, Natalka tore off the plate with his initials from the cross: his wife wanted it that way.

People think that we make a choice to die when we go to war. Some people think that we came here to Russia with our own bodies.

I had a sister with the call sign Witch. She has two school-age children, a girl and a boy. She went to the frontline because she wanted to find her place in the turbulent times and buy an apartment for her kids.

'I don't know what path they will choose for themselves. But I want them to have their own home. To know that they always have a place to come back to', she said.

This woman did nothing but create life and lay the foundation for the future. She did not sit in the headquarters, did not look for a convenient husband, but lived in dugouts and warmed herself by the stove with everyone, spent a minimum of money on herself, and saved every penny. She had a goal, and she was confidently moving towards it. This was not a person who chose war to find death.

It found her dugout. My sis Witch was burned alive.

One fellow soldier, whose name I no longer remember, said that his wife was pregnant. But he was 99 per cent happy: he wanted a boy, and the doctors said it would be a girl.

'I still don't believe it. I'm going to have a son, I know it', he said before he went on a combat mission.

We make a lot of black jokes before combat missions, and it was the same then. But I do remember something in a very low tone that differed too much from typical jokes in a crowd of good and funny soldiers.

'Hey man, what if you never have the opportunity to find out who your son or daughter really is…'

That guy with a pregnant wife just laughed. I thought, if he were a tree, it would be a saxaul. This tree has the deepest roots among plants, and it just holds on to the ground fantastically.

We were attacked very hard at the time, and that guy was the only one of all the groups who didn't come back.

The paradox is that a person does not lose their life immediately after physical death. Somewhere in the world outside of combat, they are still someone's son or daughter, brother or sister, husband or wife, friend, boyfriend or girlfriend. Relatives believe they are still alive until they see the body. It would seem that faith is a good foundation for wanting to live. But for some reason, I am sad that these families believe to the last.

I've been reacting calmly to bodies for a long time, but I feel bad realizing the fact that it is *someone's kid*. In our last days near Pisky, Donetsk region, we had thirty to forty wounded a day. I asked my comrade Koss to go to the field.

'Koss, please give me two soldiers to help me. We will at least go and collect our dead people.'

'No. I understand, but the Russians also have quadcopters with thermal cameras. I don't want to lose my only paramedic and two fighters.

I trusted him. Koss is a man who analyzes every fight and every mistake in it to avoid them in the future. Once upon a time, he told me that he ran each situation in his head like a film strip. If the three of us hadn't returned, this inner film strip of his would have been jammed from the inside until it was unbearably painful.

Of course, Koss is right. Life goes on every day and everywhere, and it doesn't care about the distance to the frontline. And if another day has come in this life, that is already a reason to take everything it offers. The funniest thing about this simple truth is that we realize it suddenly, when after two weeks on the frontline without water or a shower, we manage to wash up in warm water, do laundry, sleep in the house of some kind people who let you into their cozy bed, eat some homemade soup from some old lady who doesn't want to evacuate, or buy a whole drinking coconut in the supermarket.

What happened to that wedding ring?

I went over that ring in my hands and my life in my head. He was wrong about the size, but the truth is that this man who gave me that is one of the people I trust the most in my life. If I had to go on a very risky mission with little chance of success, I would still go with him. Not because it is crucial for our business. Not because I want to do something legendary. I would go because I'd be with him.

I didn't even have a thread to measure his finger size while he was sleeping. I cut an elastic hair band, wrapped it carefully around his ring finger, and put it against the measure on my smartphone – of course, I didn't have a ruler either.

A few days later, the ring arrived at the nearest Post Office.

'Listen, take me to the Post Office, and then we need to go to that place... Do you remember the crossroads near Nivelske? That's where we first met...' I told him, hoping he wouldn't go inside with me – military people usually are asked to show parcels for security reasons.

When I left the Post Office, my hands were shaking. We moved and started looking for this crossroad.

'Do you remember this place? Because I don't, it was winter and there are roads everywhere.'

'Okay, let it be here. The landscapes in Donbas are really the same everywhere.'

He slowed down, suddenly realizing that we're not going to meet anyone here.

I was preparing an inspirational speech, but I don't remember what I said when I proposed to him in return. But I know for sure that I could have said only one thing in different words: you are the most precious person in my life, and I want to live my life with you. Regardless of how it is made up and what fragments it consists of, you are the most important person in it.

I hope it sounded not as ridiculous as when I said 'no'. Then we tried on the rings again. Thank God, I was wrong about the size, too.

Chapter 25

MORNING

Oleksandr Komarov is a philosopher, poet, founder of the Club of Creative Philosophy project, co-author of the book **The Way of Formation of Ukrainian Identity,** *member of the board of the Ukrainian Philosophical Foundation, a Ph.D. student at the Department of Theoretical and Practical Philosophy at Taras Shevchenko National University of Kyiv.*

'May I ask something?'

'Yes, please.'

'He criticizes society so much, but what does he offer in return?'

I would be able to answer the question that Baudrillard proposes only at the end of the course, and this was only the third lecture in the cycle 'simulation and fashion', where my club and I were considering the views on the development of the society of the French sociologist and philosopher of the twentieth and twenty-first centuries, Jean Baudrillard. Our classes were held every Wednesday at 7.00 pm in a business centre in Kyiv.

Usually, there are a lot of people wandering around between the coffee machines and designer tables, minding their own business. The lounge is always noisy. Rows of offices with glass partitions: you can walk around and look at everyone as if through a screen. Not an office anthill, but a whole fair of processes, negotiations, and interviews. Everything is like on social media: everyone is beautiful, everyone sees you, but no one hears you.

But that evening we were alone in that entire space. Not a soul was around, only the administrator was bored at the reception.

Baudrillard says that there are four stages in the development of an idea. When it first emerges in society, this is the first stage. People are witnesses and active users of the idea. It is not yet distorted by anything and has an effective, 'sacramental' meaning.

The second stage is similar to the end of the honeymoon period: people lose interest somewhat, and it becomes unexciting and unprofitable for them to continue professing the idea. It's hard to serve it, to meet its high demands. It no longer seems so brilliant. Most likely this idea was born in tense or even dramatic circumstances. People are figuring out how to get around it but remain lily white. They are too lazy to change anything radically and losing touch with the old, fundamental idea does not seem like something really threatening.

The third stage is disguising the absence of an idea. This is when we collectively pretend to support the idea, but we understand that this is an imitation and that nothing remains of our original passion. There are no more direct witnesses to the idea. There is no one left who would be able to renew its original meaning. However, the basic constructions of reality are the consequences of this idea. Having lost it, we are at least forced to resort to simulating the idea – otherwise, our reality will be at risk.

The fourth stage is the final disappearance of the idea. At this stage our words and declarations no longer have any connection with actual practices. What did the creators of the idea mean? What were the actual circumstances that led to it? What are we trying to hide? No one remembers this anymore. The idea becomes a simulacrum, and our everyday life is determined by something else – something that quietly and unnoticeably replaces it. New social drivers – silence, passive consent, impersonality, empty signs, and meanings come from an unknown source and without attribution.

So, it was the evening of Wednesday, 23 February 2022. After the lecture, we traditionally went to a nearby cafe to chat. We sat over dinner for a long time and talked. Around midnight I walked home. I went to bed late at night and heard neither the air raid alarm nor the first missile strikes.

If anything, I might not have been here at all. My whole family emigrated to Germany and the United States. My relatives left the country a long time ago, but I've been a pretty bad emigrant since I was a kid.

That summer, when I was 16, I was visiting my grandparents in Kyiv and did not come back home to North Rhine-Westphalia. I wrote to my mother, German teachers, and friends that I was staying in Ukraine. I don't feel like a stranger here, I thought, but I never wrote about this to anyone. My mother immediately flew to Ukraine and tried to force me to the airport.

I stayed and wanted to make a military career in Ukraine after school. My dad, grandparents, and great-grandparents are military men. But I was discharged from the Border Guard Service with a spinal injury and that seemed to be the end of my military career.

On 25 February, no one at the military enlistment office was interested in my injuries.

'It says here that you are of limited fitness.'

'Yes.'

'Do you have any health complaints?'

'None.'

'Do you want to serve?'

'Yes.'

'Suitable for military service.'

Our brigade was formed almost entirely from scratch by volunteers, so we took into account each other's individual characteristics. For example, our commander in Kharkiv area, a beekeeper in civilian life, made a hive out of a shell box after catching a swarm of wild bees somewhere. We used to take that beehive from one firing position to another.

My comrades also treated me with understanding. They lobbied for me to become a gunner: I didn't have to carry 40 kilograms (90 pounds) of ammunition. And in one village they gave me a room in the village council so that I could be alone there and study philosophy. When it was quiet on the frontline, I would take my notes, one book in the original and the other in translation and go to the village, away from the noisy and dark dugout. I worked in a small but rather tidy office with an old table, a mirror, and a sink hanging opposite it for some reason. Before the war, when there were more people in the village, this strange room had been a social services office.

There I could have a date with my past life. Philosophy and poetry still require solitude. The creation of events and their comprehension require separate spaces. Today I have to be in the field and in the dugout and no circumstances of my own life should determine the course of fundamental comprehension – if I determine myself as a true thinker. René Descartes wrote his *Meditations on Method* not on the battlefield of the Thirty Years' War, in which he was directly involved, but much later, in the silence by his fireplace.

After all, does it really matter in which era a thinker lives if he is primarily working on the question of knowledge itself? In any case, an armed character in a Russian military uniform on the territory of Ukraine makes my work, as such, impossible. And not only because he came here with a mobile crematorium for everyone who supports the Ukrainian national idea.

They have come to enslave us spiritually and mentally because an authoritarian society does not allow freedom of thought. It's not that difficult to get on the list of people who are subject to complete destruction. I would say that it is even indecent for a Ukrainian working in the educational field not to be included. However, it is foolish to wait for your turn at the crematorium.

The Club of Creative Philosophy is almost 10 years old, and I dream of returning from the war and finishing the course of lectures on Baudrillard that I started in February 2022. To realize my dream, we need to complete in full what no one expected from us – not even ourselves.

Our independence has lost all signs of simulation.

Then, in the evening of 23 February, the audience asked me what Baudrillard was proposing, and I finally answered. He calls himself a thinker of catastrophe. The reality, which has become a ghost, collapses catastrophically. Catastrophe destroys everything, and therefore simulations as well. The surpassed catastrophe renews the meanings, cleanses our minds, and makes them flexible to perceive this life without rose-coloured glasses. It unites people with several degrees and those who have never set foot in a university. It makes us remember what we exist for as a species. It's night, after which always comes morning. Even the morning of 24 February is still morning.

AFTERWORD

If you travel through Ukraine, you will notice how diverse the country is.

Digital cities and abandoned villages with no water supply and sewage system. Noisy industrial towns and lonely houses on the slopes of the Carpathian Mountains. Fancy and gourmet restaurants facing the bombed-out walls. The ironic Odesa and pompous Lviv. Soviet high-rise buildings of Kyiv against the background of futuristic business centres. Nice households of migrant workers who go to Europe for seasonal work – sometimes more expensive than their employers' homes. Famous Ukrainian cuisine and dry galettes in bomb shelters.

Impoverished people and fabulously rich ones. Three-storey palaces with six-mat fences opposite the ancient sloping huts in the villages near Kyiv. The air-alarms and the silence of the night-time curfew. The ubiquitous hospitality of ordinary people and daily news about the power of corruption.

S-class cars which drive the bad roads and park under the front entrance, where the smell of urine cannot dissipate. Khaki-coloured military cars with shot windscreens, splashed with mud. Quiet forest oases, canyons, blue lakes, and the hum of petrol generators near coffee shops during blackouts.

Faces, exhausted with grief, and some who look as they are living their best life here and now, because tomorrow may not occur.

Transcarpathian dialect, *surzhyk* of Polissia region, Russian spoken by native Kyivites and pensioners of the capital. Nearly extinct Crimean Tatar, spoken in the annexed peninsula of Crimea. So many dialects. The broken Ukrainian of yesterday's Russian-speaking refugees who left their bombed-out towns and settled away from the missiles.

The summer heat of the Ukrainian south that burns all living things. The cold of the winter north, as if there never was and never will be spring in these lands.

Ukraine is a land of contrasts. In Ukraine, you can find the best and the worst that human nature is able to offer. This is the land of Jesus Christ and Judas Iscariot, but there are no career prospects for the apostle Peter in this society.

This is the land of people who are ready to give their lives for it, as well as the land of those who call for negotiations with terrorists.

If you only know Ukraine from the news, you know almost nothing about it.

It is the land of Kazimir Malevich and his Black Square, Mykola Leontovych and 'The Little Swallow', Ivan Pulyuy and his X-rays, etc. But it is also the land of hundreds and thousands of Ukrainian cleaners, shop assistants, and nurses with higher education who work in Europe and believe that they do not deserve any other job outside Ukraine.

This is the land of people who live in prosperity while owning nothing. The land of those who stole half the country but never recognized the wealth.

Ukraine is green and burnt.

Ukraine is friendly and angry at the same time. Ukraine loves or hates; it does not know what to do in the middle. There is white and black, but no grey. Ukraine laughs until it loses its memory, Ukraine cries endlessly.

Ukraine is strong and fragile, like crystal. Ukraine is the land of bumper harvests, but also the land of the Holodomor.

AFTERWORD

Ukraine is fighting for a better life, which is impossible under the influence of imperial Russia. Deportations, artificial famines, repression, exile, disarmament, world wars, destruction of cultural heritage, banning of the Ukrainian language, *dekulakization*, shot poets and writers, persecution, bombed cities and villages, burnt crops, flooded fields, a constant existential threat.

Ukraine died and was reborn from the ashes. Ukraine was enslaved for centuries, but it is free. Ukraine is fighting and cleansing itself. Ukraine has always fought and always will fight. So it was, is, and will be.

Thanks to all the defenders of Ukraine. Because of your efforts, I was able to write this book in a free and independent Kyiv.

Endnotes

1. Russians have almost destroyed Severodonetsk, which was the chemical industry centre of Ukraine. The critical infrastructure has been destroyed. Ninety per cent of the city has been damaged, and 80 per cent of residential buildings will have to be demolished, as they cannot be restored.
2. Redis is a nickname of Denys Prokopenko, Ukrainian officer, lieutenant colonel of the National Guard of Ukraine, commander of the Azov separate special forces detachment. On 21 September 2022, he was released from captivity as a result of a prisoner exchange. He was interned in Turkey together with the commanders of the Mariupol defenders: Svyatoslav Palamar, Oleh Khomenko, Serhii Volynskyi, and Denys Shleha. He came back to Ukraine. On 8 July 2023, Azov commanders returned to Ukraine with the consent of the Turkish side.
3. The Ukrainian military often uses the phrase 'big land' to refer to the territory of Ukraine beyond the frontline.
4. A multiple rocket launcher (MRL) or multiple launch rocket system (MLRS) is a type of rocket artillery system that contains multiple launchers which are fixed to a single platform and shoot its rocket ordnance in a fashion similar to a volley gun.
5. *Cossacks are Writing a Letter to the Turkish Sultan* is a famous painting by Ukrainian artist Ilya Repin. The subject of this painting is the well-known Letter of the Cossacks to the Turkish Sultan, written in 1676 as a response of the Cossacks to the request of the Ottoman Sultan Mehmed IV.

6. NLAW is a lightweight, shoulder-fired, and disposable (single-use) line-of-sight missile system designed for infantry use.

7. The Zaporozhian Sich was a semi-autonomous polity and proto-state of Ukrainian Cossacks that existed between the sixteenth to eighteenth centuries, including as an independent stratocratic state within the Cossack Hetmanate for over 100 years, spanning the lower Dnieper River in Ukraine.

8. In Slavic mythology, Perun is the highest god of the pantheon and the god of sky, thunder, lightning, storms, rain, law, war, fertility, and oak trees.

9. Dzharylgach is the biggest island in Ukraine and Black Sea; the biggest uninhabited island in Europe.

10. One of the developers of the cult computer game series STALKER. Volodymyr Yezhov, died at the front. He fought in the Armed Forces of Ukraine and was killed near Bakhmut in Donetsk Oblast. Volodymyr fought as part of the volunteer company UMO (Ukrainian Military Organization). The company was organized by veterans of the OUN battalion in January 2022 before Russia's full-scale invasion of Ukraine. Later, UMO fighters helped repel the Russian attack towards Kyiv.

11. Serhiy Volynskiy, alias Volyna, is the Acting Commander of the 36th Separate Marine Brigade. He took part in the Russian-Ukrainian war, participating in the defence of Mariupol. On 21 September 2022, he was released from captivity in a prisoner exchange. He was interned in Turkey together with the commanders of the Mariupol defenders: Denys Prokopenko, Sviatoslav Palamar, Oleh Khomenko, Denys Shleha. On 8 July 2023, he was returned to the territory of Ukraine.

12. Urban-type settlement in the Toretsk city municipality of Bakhmut district, Donetsk region, Ukraine. The German colony of New York was founded in 1892 on the right bank of the Kryvyi Torets River by German Mennonites.